B·L·E·S·S·I·N·G·S FOR GOD'S PEOPLE

✠ NEW EXPANDED EDITION ✠

B·L·E·S·S·IN·G·S FOR GOD'S PEOPLE

A Book of Blessings for All Occasions

Thomas G. Simons

AVE MARIA PRESS
NOTRE DAME, INDIANA 46556

~ ABOUT THE AUTHOR ~

Father Thomas G. Simons is a priest of the Diocese of Grand Rapids, Michigan. He holds a Master's Degree in Liturgy from the University of Notre Dame and served as Director of the Office for Worship in the diocese. He recently served as Executive Director of the National Federation of Priests' Council and is currently Pastor of St. Francis de Sales Parish in Muskegon, Michigan. He is also the author of *Blessings: A Reappraisal* (Resource Publications, 1981).

Excerpts from *Come, Lord Jesus* by Lucien Deiss, C.S.Sp., copyright © 1981 by Lucien Deiss, C.S.Sp., reprinted with permission of World Library Publications.

Excerpts from "Home Blessings" and "Blessing for a New School Year," copyright © Worship Resources, Inc., 3015 Zuni Street, Denver, CO 80211.

Psalm 134 from the *New American Bible,* copyright © 1970, by the Confraternity of Christian Doctrine, Washington, D.C., is used by permission of copyright owner. All rights reserved.

"Canticle of Brother Sun," translated by Benan Fahy, O.F.M., in *Writings of St. Francis of Assisi,* copyright © 1964 by Franciscan Herald Press. Used with permission of the publisher.

"Epiphany House Blessing," copyright © 1981, Office of Liturgy, Diocese of Columbus. All rights reserved.

Excerpts from *Prayers for the Domestic Church* by Edward M. Hays, copyright © 1979 by Rev. Edward M. Hays, Forest of Peace Books, Easton, KS 66020.

Excerpts from the *Book of Occasional Services* used by permission of The Church Pension Fund.

"St. Blase Service" by James Wilbur, copyright by J.S. Paluch. Used with permission of the publisher.

Excerpts reprinted from *Lutheran Book of Worship,* copyright © 1978, Augsburg Publishing House.

Excerpts from *Liturgy 70,* Christmas 1977, Liturgy Training Publications, Archdiocese of Chicago.

Excerpts from the English translation of *Rite of Baptism for Children* copyright ©1969, International Committee on English in the Liturgy, Inc. (ICEL); excerpts from the English translation of *The Roman Missal* copyright © 1973, ICEL. All rights reserved.

International Standard Book Number: 0-87793-552-1

Library of Congress Catalog Card Number: 95-76732

Cover , text design and illustrations by Katherine Robinson Coleman

Printed and bound in the United States of America.

~ DEDICATION ~
To my parents,
who have blessed me
and taught me to bless God.

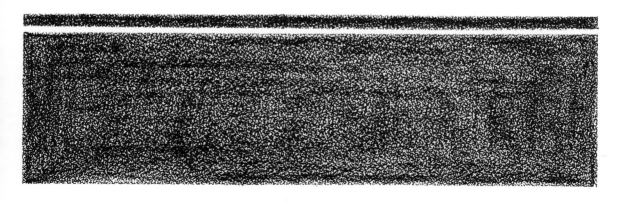

CONTENTS

Introduction ~9~

DAILY BLESSINGS ~13~

Blessing of the Morning Meal ~14~
Blessing of the Noon Meal ~15~
Blessing of the Evening Meal ~16~
Other Seasonal Meal Blessings ~17~
Morning Blessing ~24~
Night Blessing ~26~
Blessing of the Children in the Morning ~28~
Blessing of Children Before Bedtime ~29~

WEEKLY (SUNDAY) BLESSINGS ~31~

Sabbath / Sunday Meal Blessing ~32~
Blessing Before Reading Scripture ~34~
Blessing Before Worship ~34~

YEARLY BLESSINGS ~37~

Blessing of Seeds (Springtime) ~38~
Blessing of the Harvest (Autumn) ~39~
Blessing of the Advent Wreath ~41~
St. Nicholas' Day Blessing ~43~
Blessing of the Christmas Tree and Creche ~45~
Holy Family Day Blessing ~48~
New Year's Day Blessing ~50~
Epiphany House Blessing ~52~
St. Blase's Day Blessing ~53 ~
Valentine's Day Blessing ~56~
Lenten Meal Blessing ~57~
Saint Patrick's Day Blessing ~60~
Saint Joseph's Day Blessing ~62~

Palm Sunday Blessing ~64~
Holy Thursday Meal Blessing ~66~
Good Friday Meal Blessing ~68 ~
Blessing of a Family Easter Candle ~69~
Blessing of Easter Foods ~71~
Earth Day Blessing ~74~
Mother's Day Blessing ~76~
Father's Day Blessing ~77~
Labor Day Blessing ~79~
Grandparent's Day Blessing ~80~
All Saints' Day Blessing ~82~
Blessing Upon Visiting a Grave ~84~

*O*CCASIONAL BLESSINGS ~87~

Blessing of the Home ~88~
Blessing of a Vehicle ~92~
Blessing Before Travel ~93~
Blessing at the Beginning and Conclusion of a Pregnancy ~95~
Blessing of a Sick Person~97~
Blessing of an Engagement ~99~
Blessing on One's Birthday ~101~
Blessing Upon Retirement ~102~
Blessing Upon Beginning a New Job ~104~
Blessing on the Baptismal Anniversary ~105~
Blessing Upon the New School Year~107~
Blessing on an Anniversary (Marriage, Ordination Vows) ~109~
Blessing of Pets ~112~
Blessing of a Family Treasur e~114~

*B*RIEF SCRIPTURAL BLESSINGS ~117~

Notes ~125~

INTRODUCTION

The slogan on the bread wrapper boldly advertised, "Give your family the blessing of bran." I couldn't help but think that a lot of theology was being expressed in that promotional statement. We often use the word *blessing* (or *blessed*) to indicate good fortune or abundant favor. We also use it as a greeting or wish. In whatever way this word works its way into our vocabulary, it is rich in meaning and purpose.

Our Jewish ancestors knew of a deeply spiritual meaning and experience of blessing. The eighteen benedictions, which probably find their origin as eighteen suggestions, gradually became distinct blessing prayers. Hallowed by time and use, they remain a familiar part of Jewish piety and worship.

This tradition is based upon scripture which abounds with blessings. God is seen as the source of all goodness, the perfect blessing. Israel recognized this in creation, God's lasting blessing that enriches all life. God's involvement with the human person, and various persons in particular (Abraham, the prophets, kings), is marked with blessing. Blessing assumes a special place as a means of salvation in the covenant. God's people enjoyed blessing as long as they were faithful to the covenant. The scriptures admit of many variations upon the word *bless*, but basically, when the text speaks of the work of God, it means blessing; speaking of the works of persons, it means praise. The blessing of God is recognized when the human person responds with praise.

Jesus Christ is the epiphany of God's blessing in the fullness of human personhood. Jesus gives substance to God's blessing with the example of his own life. The healings, the feeding of people, the meals with his disciples—all have blessing at their foundation. Jesus identifies with the blessing tradition of his people and makes full use of it in his prayers of praise and thanksgiving.

The church, through the apostles, received this rich blessing heritage and practices it in the name of Jesus. The church calls down God's blessing upon people and upon whatever they do and whatever serves them. Blessings serve as signs; they direct our attention to God's active presence in and around us. Blessings are symbols by which we recognize God's creative power and goodness in nature and in the works of the human person. This recognition becomes the occasion to turn to God, to give thanks and praise, and call upon God for help. Blessings, therefore, imitate the sacraments. We are a people of signs, and the sacraments speak to us of decisive periods in our life when we encounter the Spirit of the living God in word and action. Blessings continue the meaning of the sacramental encounter in the course of daily living; they prolong, in a sense, the depth of the encounter and give expression to a life of faith. They offer us, at any time or moment, wherever we may be, the good news that the world and everything in it is mightily blessed by God.

The church in our time is once again recognizing the value of blessings and is anxious for them to be experienced in all areas of Christian living. The publication in English of the Roman Ritual's *Book of Blessings* in 1989 made available, especially for church leadership and parish communities, a rich resource of the church's blessing tradition. In 1988 the U.S. National Conference of Catholic Bishops published *Catholic Household Blessings and Prayers,* a treasury of models and texts gathered together especially for home and school use. In union with this aim, the following suggestions are offered as ways of recapturing and renewing the best of our blessing tradition:

1. Blessings in the life of the parish or family strengthen and celebrate the common faith of all. Many of these blessings are related to or flow from the celebration of the sacraments. For example, in the *Rite of Baptism for Children* the minister traces the sign of the cross on the forehead of the child and invites the parents and godparents to do the same. Parents may continue to make use of this blessing gesture upon their children. Likewise, parents could bless the engagement of their son or daughter by joining the families together for a blessing celebration.

2. There is a special significance to the blessings which are related to the seasons and celebrations of the church year. These seasonal blessings point out the central mysteries of faith more clearly; they bring about a closer union between believers and these mysteries. Quite simply, they bring the church into the home, school or parish, and, vice versa. Such occasions might be marked by the blessing of the Advent wreath, the Christmas tree and crèche, Easter foods, or saints'days.

3. Since Christians know that without the Lord they can do nothing, they ask for the blessing of God for themselves and for others, especially in certain life situations such as during illness, on birthdays, beginning school, an anniversary, or a journey.

4. Daily living invites the blessing of God as a recognition of the splendor of God's presence in the most ordinary moments. The blessing upon a new day, at a meal, before Sunday worship, and at night are just some of the everyday occasions to bless the Lord of blessing. Many of these blessings are prayed individually, with just a few words.

5. Things and places are blessed when, because of their particular nature or significance, they seem to be directed toward God expressing our special thanks, praise, or petition to God. They also represent our dependence upon God and our need for God's protection. Such occasions may be celebrated by the blessing of the home or apartment, a vehicle, objects of recreation, or a family treasure.

6. Any initiated Christian may celebrate a blessing. When a minister of the church is involved, it may be appropriate for that person to lead the liturgy of blessing, especially if the occasion is of a more public nature. In the family situation, the parents or another family member serves as the leader.

While by no means exhaustive or exclusive, the blessing models offered in this book touch upon many occasions in family or parochial life which are open to prayer, blessing, and celebration. I stress these as *models* because they serve as springboards for your adaptation and creativity. The blessings offered here draw upon a rich variety of sources and traditions. A basic structure, patterned upon the church's blessing practice, is always offered:

1. A call to worship or invitation to prayer

2. Reading of God's word

3. Intercessions or common prayer

4. Blessing prayer and gesture

The reading of the word especially should form an integral part of any blessing liturgy. You are always free to choose scripture passages not included here. A blessing liturgy may be simple or solemn depending upon the occasion. It should enrich the way you are already praying.

When people compose their own blessing prayer, the main components should be: praise, thanksgiving, petition/intercession, blessing. These components may be arranged in a variety of ways depending on the occasion. In the blessing gesture, the spoken word of God is made manifest. The sign of the cross, holy water, incense, and the laying on of hands in blessing are some visible expressions of the word.

The traditional meal blessing with which most Catholics are familiar begins, "Bless us, O Lord, and these thy gifts. . . ." Notice that we are first asking for a blessing upon ourselves. I hope this book will be a blessing for you and all who share it with you. St. Ambrose said it well:

> You may not be rich, you may be unable to bequeath any great possessions to your children, but one thing you can give them — the heritage of your blessing. And it is better to be blessed than to be rich.

May the richness of the Lord's blessing be upon you.

Thomas G. Simons

Daily
Blessings

ℬLESSING OF THE MORNING MEAL

All make the sign of the cross.

Leader: Blessed are you, Lord, you have nourished me from my youth. You give food to all living things. Fill our hearts with joy and cheerfulness. Give us what we need, and enough left over so that we ourselves may do good in Jesus Christ our Lord, through whom be power, glory, and honor to you forever and ever. [1]

All: **Amen.**

~or~

Leader: Give us life, Lord, through your gifts, and in your abundant goodness give us food through Christ our Lord.

All: **Amen.**

~or~

Leader: Bless, Lord, your gifts which we are about to receive from your bounty. Through Christ our Lord.[2]

All: **Amen.**

~or~

Leader: God, bless this morning meal and give to us the grace of your presence, that we may help those with whom we eat to experience the uniqueness of being loved and wanted by you, Christ, and by those who express your love.

All: **Amen.**

~or~

Leader: Lord, as we gather to share our meal make us realize our oneness in you, so that with the strength obtained from this meal we will be a source of strength for each other.

All: **Amen.**

$\mathscr{B}$LESSING OF THE NOON MEAL

~The Angelus~

Leader: The angel of the Lord spoke to Mary.

All: **And she conceived by the Holy Spirit.**

Hail Mary. . . .

Leader: I am the servant of the Lord.

All: **Let it be done to me as you say.**

Hail Mary. . . .

Leader: The Word became flesh.

All: **And made his dwelling among us.**

Hail Mary. . . .

Leader: Pray for us, holy Mother of God.

All: **Make us worthy of the promises of Christ.**

Leader: Let us pray.

Pour out your grace into our hearts, Lord! By the voice of an angel we learned of the incarnation of Christ, your Son. Lead us, by his passion and his cross to the glory of the resurrection. Through the same Christ our Lord.

All: **Amen.**

Leader: Lord, bless us as we enjoy this midday nourishment. May it refresh us as we continue our efforts this day. And may it be to your glory and honor.

All: **Amen.**

BLESSING OF THE EVENING MEAL

When all have gathered for supper, one of the family members lights a candle or candles in the center of the table.

Leader: The Lord be with you!

All: **And also with you!**

Leader: Let us give thanks to the Lord.

All: **For great is God's magnificence and glory.**

Leader: We give you thanks, God,
through your Son, Jesus Christ, our Lord,
for having enlightened us
by revealing to us the incorruptible light.
Having ended the course of this day
and reached the edge of night ,
having been filled by the light of day
which you create for our joy,
we now possess, through your kindness,
the evening light.
Therefore we praise you and glorify you
through your Son, Jesus Christ, our Lord.
Through him be glory, power, and honor,
with the Holy Spirit, now and always,
and forever and ever.[3]

All: **Amen.**

The blessing of bread follows.

Leader: You are blessed, Lord our God, king of the universe, you who have brought bread forth from the earth.[4]

~or~

Leader: Lord Jesus Christ, Bread of Angels,
living bread unto eternal life,
bless this bread
as you blessed the five loaves in the wilderness.
May all who eat it with reverence

attain through it good health
and the healing of body and spirit
which they so desired.[5]

All: **Amen.**

$\mathcal{O}$THER SEASONAL MEAL BLESSINGS

~ADVENT~

Before the meal

Leader: May the Lord Jesus come!

All: **And this world pass away.**

Leader: Father in heaven, we thank you for these days of waiting and watching for the coming of your Son, Jesus the Christ. May our hearts be filled with love, peace, and joy. We thank you and bless you for this food and drink, and all good things, through Christ our Lord.

All: **Amen.**

After the meal

Leader: Let us proclaim the Lord's coming.

All: **Eagerly we prepare to greet the Lord with joy.**

Leader: Father God, you have revived our spirits and we are grateful. Be with the poor, the lonely, the suffering. May they be blessed with the advent of our God. Through Jesus our brother.

All: **Amen.**

~CHRISTMAS~

Before the meal

Leader: The Word was made flesh. Alleluia!

All: And dwelled among us. Alleluia!

Leader: Lord our God, we thank you for the gift of your Son who is the source of all our giving. We rejoice in the splendor and glory of his coming among us. We give thanks for this food and refreshment and for all good gifts that come from you, through Christ our Lord.

All: Amen.

After the meal

Leader: All the ends of the earth have seen the saving power of our God. Alleluia!

All: The Lord has made salvation known. Alleluia!

Leader: Loving Father, you have shared the gift of your Son Jesus with us. May we share him with others, especially through our service and love for the poor, for he is the greatest gift we can give. This we ask through Jesus our Lord and brother.

All: Amen.

~EPIPHANY~

Before the meal

Leader: The kings of distant lands and from the isles bring gifts. Alleluia!

All: They come bearing precious gifts. Alleluia!

Leader: Heavenly Father, may you be enthroned upon our praises as we thank you for the King of kings, Jesus your Son. We bless you for so many gifts showered upon us, especially this food and drink before us. May we always be grateful to you, through Christ our Lord.

All: Amen.

After the meal

Leader: We see the Lord among us. Alleluia!

All:	**God has gifted each of us with himself. Alleluia!**
Leader:	Lord of all, you have made manifest your Son, Jesus Christ who is our Lord and Savior. Help us to manifest him to others, especially through our love for the unfortunate, the unwanted, and the searching. This we ask through Jesus your Son.
All:	**Amen.**

~LENT~

Before the meal

Leader:	Christ was obedient unto death, even to death on the cross.
All:	**By the cross he has redeemed the world.**
Leader:	God of infinite love, look upon us your family for whom Jesus, your Son, willingly gave his life that all might live. Bless the food of our table and nourish us ever more with the love of your Son. You live and reign with your Son forever and ever.
All:	**Amen.**

After the meal

Leader:	And I, if I am lifted up, will draw all people to myself.
All:	**By the cross he has redeemed the world.**
Leader:	We praise and thank you, Father, for the sacrifice of your Son, Jesus Christ. May his body, broken for us, and his blood, poured out for us, cause us to be eucharist for others. Help us to share the victory of the cross with all who suffer and are persecuted. We make our prayer through Christ our Lord.
All:	**Amen.**

~HOLY WEEK~

Before the meal

Leader:	Jesus Christ is the light of the world.
All:	**A light no darkness can extinguish.**
Leader:	Powerful God, your Son Jesus entered the darkness of death and rose victorious as the light of hope for the world. We bless you with

uplifted hearts and hands, and rejoice in the blessings around us, especially this good food. We come to you in Jesus, the Lamb slain for sinners.

All: **Amen.**

After the meal

Leader: Jesus Christ is victor!

All: **Christ has died, Christ is risen, Christ will come again.**

Leader: Blessed are you, God our Father, for you have blessed us with your Son, Jesus. He is the Lamb who has been slain for our sins and has won for us the freedom to be his brothers and sisters. May our praise give you glory and cause us to share you and your Son with all who struggle for freedom. We ask this through Christ our Lord.

All: **Amen.**

~EASTER~

Before the meal

Leader: The Lord is risen, alleluia, alleluia!

All: **He is truly risen, alleluia, alleluia!**

Leader: Glorious Father, we rejoice that your Son and our brother, Jesus, is victorious over sin and death. Bless this good food that we share as we rejoice in his victory and give us the strength to share the good news of Easter with others. We ask this through Jesus Christ risen, now and forever.

All: **Amen.**

After the meal

Leader: Jesus Christ has been raised, alleluia, alleluia!

All: **We rejoice in his victory, alleluia, alleluia!**

Leader: Almighty God, we thank you for blessing us with your Son Jesus. As we have rejoiced with him in this meal may our hearts long for the new and eternal banquet with Christ our risen brother. Help us to share the blessings of this table with others. Through Christ the risen Lord.

All: **Amen.**

~ASCENSION~

Before the meal

Leader: The Lord will return, alleluia!

All: **Just as he has said, alleluia!**

Leader: God our Savior, we rejoice in the ascension of your Son who is our glory and our hope. May your blessing be upon us as we share this nourishment. Let this food aid our desire to share the heavenly banquet with Jesus the Christ in the eternal kingdom, forever and ever.

All: **Amen.**

After the meal

Leader: God is with us always, alleluia!

All: **To the end of time, alleluia!**

Leader: Father, in this meal we have a taste of the friendship that you have shown to us in your Son Jesus. Help and strengthen us to follow Christ more closely and to uplift others in his life and love. We make this prayer in the name of Jesus.

All: **Amen.**

~PENTECOST~

Before the meal

Leader: Come, Creator Spirit.

All: **Fill us with your love.**

Leader: Father, we thank you for the gift of the Spirit poured out upon us. We ask you to bless us with the food we share. May it enliven our spirit. May we always hunger for the gifts and fruits of the Spirit and share your abundance with hearts full of love and gratitude. We make our prayer through Jesus and the Creator Spirit, always and ever.

All: **Amen.**

After the meal

Leader: The Spirit of the Lord is upon us.

All: **God's love is in our hearts.**

Leader: Father in heaven, you have blessed us with your living and loving Spirit. May the food we have shared invigorate us and cause us to share the blessings of the Spirit with everyone around us. Help us to radiate the warmth of the Spirit in all we do. We ask this through Jesus, in the power of the Spirit, now and always.

All: **Amen.**

~MARIAN FEAST~

Before the meal

Leader: Hail Mary, full of grace.

All: **The Lord is with you.**

Leader: Lord God, we praise and thank you for Mary, the mother of your Son, Jesus. Bless our food and our conversation on this feast of *(name the occasion).* May we rejoice with Mary and her son, Jesus the Christ, now and always.

All: **Amen.**

After the meal

Leader: Blessed is the fruit of your womb.

All: **Blessed be Jesus forever.**

Leader: Loving God, we rejoice today with Mary who was chosen from among all women to be the mother of your Son. May we follow her example and take her advice to do whatever he tells us. Bless all our loved ones and the brothers and sisters we do not know. Through Christ our Lord.

All: **Amen. Hail Mary . . .**

~PATRON SAINT DAY~

Before the meal

Leader: You are praised in your saints.

All: **And glorified in their witness.**

Leader: Lord our God, today we honor *(name the family member, friend or guest)* who celebrates his/her name day, the feast of *(name the saint or patron)*. Bless this meal in which we keep festival with the holy ones who gave you praise through their life. May we give you praise now with Christ and his saints forevermore.

All: **Amen.**

After the meal

Leader: Blessed be the saints of God.

All: **Theirs is the crown of life.**

Leader: Father in heaven, we thank you for your presence on this day of St. *(name the saint or patron)*. May our celebration stir in us a desire to share in the friendship of the holy men, women, and children who loved you in life and who are an example to us. We make our prayer in the name of Jesus.

All: **Amen.**

~THANKSGIVING~

Before the meal

Leader: The earth has yielded its fruit.

All: **God, our God, has blessed us.**

Leader: Father, God of goodness, you have given us this land and made it fruitful through the work of human hands. Bless this harvest of plenty. May it sustain our lives and draw us more closely to one another and to you in thanksgiving and praise. We make our prayer through Jesus Christ.

All: **Amen.**

Leader:	Give thanks always and everywhere.
All:	**To the Father in the name of Jesus.**
Leader:	Lord, we thank you for your many gifts and praise you as the source of all we have and are. Teach us to acknowledge always your blessings around us and to be thankful for the infinite expressions of your love. Help us to be generous with others as you are generous with us. We come to you in praise and thanksgiving through Jesus your Son.
All:	**Amen.**

*M*ORNING BLESSING

Rise and face the east, making the sign of the cross on the forehead, lips, and breast. Pray:

I thank you, everliving God, for
reawakening my soul. Great is
your mercy and your faithfulness.[6]

Then pray the Canticle of Brother Sun:

Most high, all-powerful, all good, Lord!
    All praise is yours, all glory, all honor
    And all blessing.

To you, alone, Most High, do they belong.
    No mortal lips are worthy
    To pronounce your name.

All praise be yours, my Lord, through all that you have made,
    And first my lord Brother Sun,
    Who brings the day; and light you give to us through him.

How beautiful is he, how radiant in all his splendor!
    Of you, Most High, he bears the likeness.

All praise be yours, my Lord, through Sister Moon and Stars;

In the heavens you have made them, bright
And precious and fair.

All praise be yours, my Lord, through Brothers Wind and Air,
And fair and stormy, all the weather's moods,
By which you cherish all that you have made.

All praise be yours, my Lord, through Sister Water,
So useful, lowly, precious and pure.

All praise be yours, my Lord, through Brother Fire,
Through whom you brighten up the night.
How beautiful is he, how gay! Full of power and strength.

All praise be yours, my Lord, through Sister Earth, our mother,
Who feeds us in her sovereignty and produces
Various fruits with colored flowers and herbs.

All praise be yours, my Lord, through those who grant pardon,
For love of you; through those who endure
Sickness and trial.

Happy those who endure in peace,
By you, Most High, they will be crowned.

All praise be yours, my Lord, through Sister Death,
From whose embrace no mortal can escape.

Woe to those who die in mortal sin!
Happy those she finds doing your will!
The second death can do no harm to them.

Praise and bless my Lord, and give him thanks,
And serve him with great humility.[7]

—*St. Francis of Assisi*

NIGHT BLESSING

Before retiring, face the east and with hands raised, pray:

Come, bless the LORD,
all you servants of the LORD
who stand by night in the house of the LORD!
Lift up your hands to the holy place
and bless the LORD.
May the LORD, maker of heaven and earth
bless you from Zion.

—Psalm 134, NRSV

~or~

Blessed are you, Lord, God of all creation
for you make the bonds of sleep to fall upon my eyes
and slumber on my eyelids.
May it be your will,
O Lord my God and God of my ancestors,
to allow me to lie down in peace
and to let me rise up again in peace.
Let not my thoughts trouble me, nor fearful dreams,
but let my rest be perfect before you.[8]

~or~

Blessed be the Lord by day!
Blessed be the Lord by night!
Blessed be the Lord when we lie down!
Blessed be the Lord when we rise up!
For in your hands are all the souls of all the living and dead.
Into your hands, I commend my spirit.
You have redeemed me, O Lord God of truth.[9]

Then conclude with the Divine Praises.

> Blessed be God.
> Blessed be God's holy name.
> Blessed be Jesus Christ, true God and true man.
> Blessed be the name of Jesus.
> Blessed be his most sacred heart.
> Blessed be his most precious blood.
> Blessed be Jesus in the most holy sacrament of the altar.
> Blessed be the Holy Spirit, the Consoler.
> Blessed be the great Mother of God, Mary most holy.
> Blessed be her holy and immaculate conception.
> Blessed be her glorious assumption.
> Blessed be the name of Mary, virgin and mother.
> Blessed be St. Joseph, her most chaste spouse.
> Blessed be God in his angels and in his saints.

Seal the night prayer by making the sign of the cross.

ℬLESSING OF CHILDREN IN THE MORNING

As children prepare to go to school or a daily activity, all come together.

~GATHERING PRAYER~

Leader: Jesus loved children and blessed them.
Imitating Jesus, I/we bless you
as you go your way.
May Jesus stay with you, protect you,
and lead you safely
back home.

All: **Amen.**

~SCRIPTURE READING~

If time permits, a brief scriptural reading may be offered (see pp. 118-124).

~INTERCESSIONS~

The leader may invite the child (children) to express praise for God, as is the church's practice at morning prayer. Such acclamation can be:

Praise God!
Bless the Lord!
Give praise to Jesus!
Wonderful is our God!
Glory be to Christ!

After each acclamation all may respond:

Amen!

~SENDING PRAYER~

The leader may make the sign of the cross on the forehead of the child, saying, "(Name), Go with God," before all go their way.

*B*LESSING OF CHILDREN BEFORE BEDTIME

As children's bedtime approaches, all gather together. The sign of the cross is made.

~GATHERING PRAYER~

Leader: As this day comes to a close, we give thanks to God for all blessings, seen and unseen. As you sleep and find rest for your body and mind, may you be strengthened in the hope of a new day and give praise for God's goodness.

All: **Amen.**

~SCRIPTURE READING~

If the leader so chooses, a brief scriptural prayer may be offered (see pp. 118-124).

~INTERCESSIONS~

The leader may invite the child or other family members to give thanks to God for people, events, or blessings experienced that day. These expressions can be summed up by praying together either the Lord's Prayer, the Hail Mary, or the Glory Be. The Act of Contrition, especially during Lent, may also be prayed together.

~BLESSING GESTURE~

The leader may then sprinkle the children with holy water (or Easter water brought home from the church's font, during the Easter season), or make the sign of the cross on the forehead of the child as they go to bed.

Weekly (Sunday) Blessings

$\mathscr{S}$ABBATH / SUNDAY MEAL BLESSING

Sabbath (Friday sundown to Saturday sundown) and Sunday (Saturday sundown to Sunday sundown) together form the week's fullness and beginning, and are special days for Jews and Christians.

As we sit down at the table on the Sabbath we especially pray in union with our Jewish brothers and sisters.

When the family has gathered at the table, the mother or another in the family lights the candle and says:

> God of Creation, we welcome the evening with the light. May it help us to recognize the Son of Justice who is the Light of the World. Let it dispel every kind of darkness and keep us in the warmth of your love. Amen.

All pray silently for a few moments.

Leader: The Lord bless us and keep us.

All: **Amen.**

Leader: The Lord let his light shine upon us.

All: **Amen.**

Leader: The Lord grant us health and peace.

All: **Amen.**

Leader: We thank you, our Father,
for the life and knowledge
which you have revealed to us through
Jesus your Son.

All: **Glory be yours through all ages.**

Leader: Just as bread broken
was scattered on the hills,
then was gathered and became one,
so as we gather may we be made one,
for yours is glory and power through all ages.[10]

All: **Amen.**

The leader prays over the bread:

> Blessed are you, Lord God of all creation.
> Through your goodness we have this bread to eat,
> which earth has given
> and human hands have made.
> Let it become for us a source of nourishment and strength.[11]

All: **Blessed be God forever.**

The bread is broken and shared by all. If wine is shared, it is blessed as the leader prays:

> Blessed are you, Lord, God of all creation.
> Through your goodness we have this wine to drink,
> which earth has given
> and human hands have made.
> Let it become for us a source of refreshment and joy.[12]

All: **Blessed be God forever.**

The cup is passed and shared by all.

On Sunday, after the meal is finished, the leader prays:

> Great God who raised Jesus from death to life,
> raise us up in a spirit of freedom and holiness.
> May the life of Christ shine forth in each us
> as we bless you for the goodness of this day.
> We pray in the name of the resurrected one,
> Jesus, who lives and rules with you,
> now and forever.

All: **Amen.**

All may exchange a sign of Christ's peace and love dwelling among us.

BLESSING BEFORE READING SCRIPTURE

Make the sign of the cross on the forehead, lips and breast. Pray:

> Blessed Lord, who caused all the holy scriptures to be written for our learning: Grant that we may in such wise hear them, read, mark, learn and inwardly digest them, that by patience and comfort of the holy word, we may embrace and ever hold fast the blessed hope of everlasting life, which you have given us in our Savior Jesus Christ. Amen.[13]

Read the scriptures, perhaps the readings to be proclaimed at Sunday eucharist. (If more than one person is present, the group could discuss the readings.) A period of reflective silence would also be appropriate. Place the book of the scriptures on a table between a candle and some burning incense, if desired.

Before taking leave the scriptures may be reverenced with a kiss.

BLESSING BEFORE WORSHIP

Gather briefly for prayer before the Sunday eucharist. Begin with a renewal of baptismal promises:

All: Lord Jesus Christ, you are the king of the whole world.
All that was made was created for you.
Exercise your sovereign rights over me.
I renew my baptismal vows
renouncing Satan with all his works and his false glamor,
and I promise to live as a good Christian.
In particular, I pledge myself to do all in my power
to make the rights of God and of your church triumph in the world.
Divine Heart of Jesus,

**I offer you whatever I do, however feeble,
to obtain that all human hearts may admit your sacred kingship,
so that the kingdom of your peace will be established
throughout the whole world.** **Amen.**[14]

—Pope Pius XI

Sprinkle everyone with holy water. Then one of the parents or another person prays:

Almighty God, you pour out on all who desire it the spirit of grace and supplication. Deliver us, as we come into your presence, from cold hearts and wandering thoughts, that with steady minds and burning zeal we may worship you in spirit and in truth; through your Son, Jesus Christ our Lord.[15]

All: **Amen.**

~or~

O Lord, on this the lord of days, we ask you to open our minds and hearts to receive your word and to make us thankful as we celebrate the memorial of your Son. As we blend with the larger body of your church, may we go forth in the joy and peace of your risen Son Jesus.

All: **Amen.**

Parents may lay hands upon their children and bless each in their own words, or they may say:

Bless us, O God, with a reverent sense of your presence, that we may be at peace and may worship you with all our minds and spirit, through Jesus Christ our Lord.[16]

All: **Amen.**

Yearly
Blessings

*B*LESSING OF SEEDS (SPRINGTIME)

As springtime approaches seeds may be blessed before planting.

The prayer leader greets all present and invites them to join in the blessing celebration.

~CALL TO WORSHIP~

Leader: Let us bless the Lord of all times and seasons.

All: **And give thanks and praise.**

Leader: Let us listen to the Lord's word. One of those present reads one of the following scripture passages:

~WORD SERVICE~

Genesis 1:11-12	Genesis 2:4-9,15
Isaiah 55:10-11	Matthew 13:1-9
John 12:24-26 2	Corinthians 9:8-11
1 Corinthians 3:4-9	

The prayer leader may offer some brief reflections on the proclaimed word. Others may offer prayers of thanksgiving recognizing the goodness of God in creation. Then pray the blessing prayer.

~BLESSING PRAYER~

Leader: Praise to you, Lord our God, for you bring forth life from the earth. We ask you to bless these seeds that hold the promise of life. Send sunshine and showers to nurture their growth. Watch over these seeds so they grow to maturity. Help us to share the food, the fruit of these seeds, with all our sisters and brothers. We ask this in Jesus' name.

All: **Amen.**

Leader: Lord, we pray, bless these seeds and nurture them with good soil, strengthen them in the gentle movement of the wind, refresh them with rain from the heavens, and let them grow to full maturity for the good of body and soul. We ask this through Christ our Lord.[17]

All: **Amen.**

The seeds may be sprinkled with holy water. Then pray the Lord's Prayer together.

ℬLESSING OF THE HARVEST (AUTUMN)

As fruits and vegetables reach the conclusion of their natural season, pause to give thanks for the fruitfulness of the earth.

The prayer leader reminds those gathered of the occasion for the blessing celebration.

~CALL TO WORSHIP~

Leader: The Lord is bounteous with blessings.

All: **To God belongs our thanksgiving.**

Leader: The word of the Lord speaks to us.

~WORD SERVICE~

Read one or more of the following scriptures:

Genesis 8:20-22   Joel 2:21-24, 26-27

Deuteronomy 8:7-18   Isaiah 55:8-12

Luke 12:15-21

Discuss the passage or passages and their meaning for today, if desired. Some of those gathered may offer thanksgiving prayers recognizing the handiwork of God in his creation. Then pray the blessing prayer.

~BLESSING PRAYER~

Leader: Lord, Bounteous God, you do not cease to give many riches in the rain that falls from heaven and nourishment for life in the fertility of soil. We give thanks to you for the fruits of the land which we have harvested, and we pray that you bless and preserve these fruits which we have received from your hand. Help us to be mindful of the needs of others as we rejoice in the bounty of your goodness to us. We make this prayer through Christ our Lord.[18]

All: **Amen.**

~or~

Leader: Lord, maker of all things, you open your hand and satisfy the desire of every living creature. We praise you for crowning the fields with your blessings and enabling us once more to gather in the fruits of the earth. Teach us to use your gifts carefully, that our land may continue to yield her increase; through your Son, Jesus Christ our Lord.[19]

All: **Amen.**

ℬLESSING OF THE ADVENT WREATH

This celebration is for a simple Advent wreath blessing in the home (or, with slight adaptation, in the classroom).

Gather around the Advent wreath before the evening meal on Saturday and make the sign of the cross.

Parent: The Lord of Light has come to save us.

All: **Let us live in God's light.**

Parent: Let us pray.

God, our Father in heaven, by your word all things are made holy. Send forth your blessing upon this Advent wreath, and grant that we who use it may prepare our hearts and minds well for the coming of your Son Jesus. May we receive from you many blessings and graces for our family. We ask these things in the name of the same Christ, your Son, our Lord and Brother.

All: **Amen.**

Say the prayer of the week. Then light the candle.

~FIRST WEEK~

Parent: O Lord, stir up your might and come! Be our protector and liberator; rescue us from the dangers that threaten us because of our sins, and lead us to our salvation. You live and reign forever and ever.

All: **Amen.**

One candle is lighted by the youngest child and left burning during the meal.

~SECOND WEEK~

Parent: Lord, stir up our hearts to prepare the way of your only-begotten Son so that through his coming on earth we may serve you always with a pure intention. You live and reign forever and ever.

All: **Amen.**

Two candles are lighted by the oldest child and left burning during the meal.

~THIRD WEEK~

Parent: Hear our prayers, Lord, and enlighten the darkness of our minds by your coming on earth. You live and reign forever and ever.

All: **Amen.**

Three candles are lighted by the mother or another child and left burning during the meal.

~FOURTH WEEK~

Parent: Lord, stir up your might and come! Aid us with your powerful assistance so that through your grace and merciful forgiveness we may attain salvation, which now is hindered by our sins. You live and reign forever and ever.

All: **Amen.**

All four candles are lighted by the father or another child and left burning during the meal.

~CHRISTMAS DAY~

Light all the candles, including a white candle placed in the center of the wreath.

Parent: Father,
we are filled with new light
by the coming of your Word among us.
May the light of faith
shine in our words and actions.
Grant this through our Lord Jesus Christ, your Son, who lives and reigns with you and the Holy Spirit, one God, forever and ever.[20]

All: **Amen.**

ℋT. NICHOLAS' DAY BLESSING

St. Nicholas is the source for many of our present Christmas customs, especially that of gift giving. His feast is an appropriate time to express the spiritual aspects of giving and sharing and invites a celebration of blessing in his memory.

~CALL TO WORSHIP~

Leader: I will look after my sheep, says the Lord.

All: And I will raise up a shepherd to pasture them.

~or~

Leader: The Spirit of the Lord was upon him.

All: To bring good news to the poor and to heal the brokenhearted.

Leader: Let us pray.

All powerful God,
you made St. Nicholas a bishop and leader of the church
to inspire your people with his teaching and example.
May we give fitting honor to his memory
and always have the assistance of his prayers.
We ask this through our Lord Jesus Christ, your Son,
who lives and reigns with you and the Holy Spirit,
one God, forever and ever.[21]

All: Amen.

~WORD SERVICE~

1 Peter 5:1-4   Hebrews 13:7-9a

The following summary of the life of St. Nicholas may be read and discussed.

St. Nicholas was born in Asia Minor. He was named bishop of Myra, a poor and run-down diocese. When his wealthy parents died, he gave his wealth to the poor and devoted himself to the conversion of sinners.

Once he heard that a man who had become very poor intended to abandon his three daughters to prostitution because he could not afford a dowry for them to be married. Nicholas, the story goes, on three occasions threw a bag of gold through the window into the room of the sleeping father. His daughters soon were married. Later the father came to Nicholas, fell at his feet and said, "Nicholas, you are my helper. You have delivered my soul and my daughters' souls from hell."

This story and his many other works of charity led to the tradition of giving presents on Nicholas' feast day and at Christmas in his name. The name Santa Claus, in fact, evolved from his name.

Nicholas died at Myra in 350. His popularity, already great, increased when his relics were brought to Bari, Italy, in 1087. Both the Eastern and Western churches honor him. St. Nicholas is the patron saint of Russia, Greece, Apulia, Sicily, and Lorraine. He is regarded as the special patron of children. His feast is December 6.

~INTERCESSIONS~

Reader: For the gift of each person here.

All: **We give thanks.**

Reader: For the capacity to care for and to share with those in need.

All: **We give thanks.**

Reader: For a holiday season of joy, hope, and peace.

All: **We give thanks.**

~BLESSING PRAYER~

Leader: Gracious and good Lord, we bless you on this feast of St. Nicholas, your servant, who is an example to us of a life of charity and love. May we see in his life an invitation to imitate his good deeds. Make us always mindful of the needs of others and help us rejoice in the abundance of your goodness around us. Through Jesus our Lord.

All: **Amen.**

Share a special treat or exchange small gifts, if desired.

$\mathcal{B}$LESSING OF THE CHRISTMAS TREE AND CRÈCHE

Blessing of the Christmas Tree[22]

A Christmas tree affirms life in seasons of cold and gloom. By decorating it with objects that have been gathered over the years a family says something about its own special life. When decorated, the tree is a blessing to the home and deserves our blessing in return.

Decorate the tree, but ask each person to save one favorite ornament (or make a new one) to put on at the blessing. When the tree is complete, but before turning on its lights, gather the family for a simple blessing. One person should prepare the brief scripture reading beforehand.

~CALL TO WORSHIP~

Leader: We come here to pray in the name of the Father and of the Son and of the Holy Spirit.

All: Amen.

~WORD SERVICE~

Psalm 96:11-12 or Ezekiel 17:22-24

Then, one by one, put an ornament on the tree saying:

May this Christmas tree bring the blessing of (*mention the blessing desired for the family or the world*).

~BLESSING PRAYER~

Leader: Let us pray.

Holy Lord and eternal God, you caused your Son, our Lord Jesus Christ, to be planted like a tree of life in your church by being born of the Blessed Virgin Mary. We ask you to bless this tree that all who see it may be filled with a holy desire to be grafted as living branches onto the same Lord Jesus Christ, who lives and reigns with you, in the unity of the Holy Spirit, God, forever and ever.

All:	**Amen.**

~or~

Leader:	All glory and praise to you, heavenly Father. We thank you for sending us your Son Jesus to be our brother. Bless us as we gather here, and bless our Christmas tree. Let its lights remind us of Jesus, who is the light of the world. Father, we love you, and we praise you through Christ our Lord.
All:	**Amen.**

~or~

Leader:	Father in heaven, we thank you for your goodness. Bless this tree that we have decorated in honor of your Son's birth among us. Let its lights remind us that he is Lord, and its decorations recall our joy. Grant that we may receive him as our savior, and continue to give you glory by our lives. We ask this, Father, in the name of Christ our Lord.
All:	**Amen.**

~or~

Leader:	Lord of the forest, maker of trees, we honor you as we dedicate this tree that it be a sign of Christmas. Green as life are its branches; soft as compassion are its needled leaves; strong as love is its trunk. May all trees be for us Christmas trees and trees of life. As sons and daughters of Adam and Eve, let us rejoice in this tree of life; may the spirit of kindness and love rest upon it. [23]
All:	**Amen.**

Exchange a sign of peace. Then turn on the lights and sing a verse of "O Come, O Come, Emmanuel."

Blessing of the Crèche[24]

On Christmas Eve gather the family together and set up the nativity scene except for the figure of the infant. Turn out the lights and sit quietly in darkness for some moments. Then, as one begins lighting the candles around the crèche or around the room if the creche is under the Christmas tree, all hum or sing "O Come, O Come, Emmanuel." Emphasize the refrain, "Rejoice, rejoice. . . ."Tell the Christmas story or read it from Luke 2. Place the infant in the crib at the proper moment. Sing "Silent Night" or another favorite carol, then pray.

Leader: We praise you, Lord God of all creation, for you have brought us to this season of rejoicing, and have given us the story of the birth of Jesus. Through all the days of Christmas may these figures that tell that story be blessed, and may this place be filled with hospitality, joy, gentleness, and thanksgiving to you. We ask this in the name of Jesus the Lord.

All: **Amen.**

~or~

Leader: Blessed are you, Lord God, king of all creation. We praise you for your love. We thank you because you have loved us so much that you sent your only Son to bring us eternal life. Bless this nativity scene that we have prepared, and let it be a reminder to us of the Lord Jesus, Son of God and Son of Mary. Father, we praise you through Christ our Lord.

All: **Amen.**

~or~

Leader: Heavenly Father, accept our thanks for all that you have done for us. May this scene of Christ's birth remind us of his love for you and for us. Fill our hearts with the faith of the shepherds and the peace of which the angels sang so that we may always understand Christmas as beginning and ending with Christ, our Redeemer.

All: **Amen.**

~or~

Leader: Lord, we pray before this Christmas crib, and await the feast of the birth of the Holy Child. Call forth the child from within each of us; cause us to wonder and to rejoice again in this most ancient feast. With the shepherds we come to the birth of Christ, seeking a simple celebration. The greatest gift will be ourselves given to you, Our God, and to each other. May the star of Bethlehem which shone brightly over the first crib stand guard over us filling us and all the earth with light and peace.[25]

All: **Amen.**

The Christmas tree and crèche can be sprinkled with holy water. Then join in singing Christmas carols.

ℋOLY FAMILY DAY BLESSING

On this feast pause to thank and bless the Lord for calling all families, like the holy family of Nazareth, to be one in God's love.

~CALL TO WORSHIP~

Leader: Come, let us bless the Lord.

All: **And praise God's name.**

Leader: Let us pray.

> God, our Father and our Mother, we thank you for the family of Mary, Joseph, and Jesus. It was at home with his parents that Jesus grew in wisdom and age and your grace, that he learned to know the Law and the prophets and to do right and love goodness. Bless with strength and patience and good humor all who would make such homes today. We ask this in the name of Jesus the Lord.

~WORD SERVICE~

Read one of the following scripture passages:

Sirach 3:2-6

Matthew 2:13-15,19-23

Luke 2:41-52

Colossians 3:12-21

Luke 2:22-40 or 2:22,39-40

Follow the reading with a litany of petitions:

Leader: We now pray together that our many families may reflect the charity of the holy family and may be signs of God's saving presence in the world.

That we may always remember that our individual families are each a part of the family of man, and that we may have concern for one another.

All:	**We pray to the Lord.**
Leader:	For our nation (*say the name of your country*) which has given us so many advantages and so much of the goods of the world.
All:	**We pray to the Lord.**
Leader:	For families who are poor, who are hungry, who suffer from war or disease.
All:	**We pray to the Lord.**
Leader:	That all of us, members of Christian families, may follow our own proper path to holiness and sustain one another in grace throughout our lives.
All:	**We pray to the Lord.**
Leader:	For the members of our families who are not with us today and for those whom God has called to himself.
All:	**We pray to the Lord.**

Other petitions may be added. Conclude with the Our Father, Hail Mary and Glory Be.

~BLESSING PRAYER~

Leader:	Father, help us to live as the holy family, united in respect and love. Bring us to the joy and peace of your eternal home. Grant this through our Lord Jesus Christ, your Son, who lives and reigns with you and the Holy Spirit, one God, forever and ever.[26]
All:	**Amen.**

The members of the family then bless each other with a sign of the cross on the forehead and share a hug.

NEW YEAR'S DAY BLESSING

The beginning of a new year can be an appropriate time to ask God's blessings upon a new period of time in life.

Gather before the meal. All join in making the sign of the cross.

~CALL TO WORSHIP~

Leader: Let us bless the Lord of days.

All: **To God belong the times and the seasons.**

Leader: Let us pray.

O God our Creator, you have divided our life into days and seasons, and called us to acknowledge your providence year after year. Accept your people who come to offer their praises and, in your mercy, receive their prayers. Through Christ our Lord.[27]

All: **Amen.**

~WORD SERVICE~

Read one of the following scripture passages:

> Ecclesiastes 3:1-15   Psalm 90
> 2 Corinthians 5:17; 6:2   Revelation 21:1-14, 22-24

A brief litany of thanksgiving follows:

Leader: For the blessings, seen and unseen, of this past year.

All: **We thank you, Lord.**

Leader: For the gift of life and its fullness.

All: **We thank you, Lord.**

Leader: For the wisdom to number our days in the presence of our God.

All: **We thank you, Lord.**

Other thanksgiving prayers may be added. Conclude them with the Lord's Prayer.

~BLESSING PRAYER~

Leader: *(with hands extended over the family members)*

Eternal Father, you have placed us in a world of space and time, and through the events of our lives you bless us with your love. Grant that in this new year we may know your presence, see your love at work, and live in the light of the event which gives us joy forever—the coming of your Son, Jesus Christ our Lord.[28]

All: Amen.

The leader lays hands on each person and signs his or her forehead with the cross. If desired, bless family and individual calendars with the following prayer:

Leader: Lord, you who live outside of time and reside in the imperishable moment, we ask your blessing this New Year upon your gift to us of time. Bless our calendars, these ordered lists of days, weeks, and months, of holidays, holy days, fasts, and feasts. May they remind us of birthdays and other gift-days as they teach us the secret that all life is meant for celebration and contemplation. Bless, Lord, this new year, each of its days and nights. Bless us with happy seasons and long life. Grant to us, Lord, the New Year's gift of a year of love.[29]

All: Amen.

𝒠PIPHANY HOUSE BLESSING [30]

Leader: Peace be in this place.

All: **And with all who enter here.**

~THANKSGIVING OVER THE WATER~

Leader: Blessed are you, Lord, God of all creation. You have blessed the earth with abundant water. May it be for us a pledge of cleansing and protection.

All: **Blessed be God forever.**

A member of the family takes the water and a sprig of greenery and sprinkles the rooms of the house and the people, while all say together:

All: **I will pour out water upon the thirsty ground,
and streams upon the dry land;
I will pour out my spirit upon your offspring,
and my blessing upon your descendants.**

~THE INSCRIPTION~

19 + C M B + 9___ (year)

One person makes the inscription with chalk above the door, while another proclaims the corresponding words.

The three wisemen,

C	Caspar,
M	Melchior, and
B	Balthasar
	followed the star of God's Son who became man
19	one thousand, nine hundred, and
9___	ninety-(*year*) years ago.
+	May Christ bless our dwelling
+	and remain with us throughout the new year.

~ACCLAMATION~

Leader: Lift up your heads, O gates!

All: That the King of Glory may come in.

Leader: Who is the King of Glory?

All: The Lord of hosts is the King of Glory!

~PRAYER~

Leader: God of Salvation, incline your ear.
Bless us and all those who are gathered here.
Your angel send us,
Who will defend us,
And fill with grace
All who dwell in this place.

All: Amen.

$\mathscr{S}$T. BLASE'S DAY BLESSING [31]

Read and discuss the story of St. Blase.

Blase, a physician who later became a bishop, died for the faith in 316. While in prison he healed a child who nearly died because of a fish bone in the throat. Due to this and other cures, people pray to him as a helper in sickness. The devotion spread from the Near East to Europe in the 800s; he became one of the most popular saints during the Middle Ages.

In central Europe and the Latin countries people receive a blessed bread stick on St. Blase's Day. They eat a bit of it whenever they have a sore throat. In Italy and Ireland it is customary to bless oil in honor of St. Blase. The priest touches people's throats with a dab of the oil, and they take some home for use when they are ill. The best known custom, the blessing of throats, has been in use for centuries.

The priest holds crossed candles under the chin or over the head of each person and says a prayer of blessing.

The legendary details of St. Blase's life and these customs grew out of faith in God and belief in the church's concern for human suffering. The blessing given this day is the church's gift to us. It asks God's care for our safety and health, and conveys the message of his fatherly love in our daily needs.

Perhaps the European custom of giving blessed bread (or oil, wine, water and fruit) can be adapted when blessing children. Some nuts, a small piece of fruit, or hard candy given to the children after the blessing may remind them to thank God for the mouth and throat through which they breathe and speak, taste and swallow, and also serve as a reminder to care for the mouth and throat properly.

A song of praise may be sung by all.

~GREETING~

Leader: The favor of the Lord Jesus be with you.

All: **And also with you.**

~WORD SERVICE~

Reader: James 5:14-16 or 1 Kings 17:17-24
                         Sirach 7:33-36
                         2 Corinthians 4:10-18
                         Matthew 8:14-17
                         Matthew 9:1-8
                         Luke 7:1-10
                         Matthew 4:23-25
                         John 5:1-8

~HOMILY~

It may be helpful to explain that the blessing is a sign of thanks for our throats, by which we breathe and speak, taste and swallow.

All come forward to receive the blessing from the parent or leader who lays hands on each person and says:

> *(Name)*, may God preserve you by the prayers of St. Blase from sore throats and all illness. Through Christ our Lord.

Response: Amen.

~INTERCESSIONS~

Remember others who are sick and in need of healing prayer.

Leader: For (*name or names*), we pray to the Lord.

All: Lord, hear our prayer.

~CLOSING PRAYER AND BLESSING~

Leader: Ever living God, we celebrate the memory of St. Blase who died in witness to the gospel. Give us also the courage to be faithful in your service and the final joy of glory with you. We ask this through Christ our Lord.

All: Amen.

Leader: Every worthwhile gift comes from above.
May God grant you health of mind and body,
and strengthen you with every grace and blessing,
that you may enjoy his favor in everlasting life.

All: Amen.

Leader: Blessed be the Lord.

All: Now and forever.

$\mathcal{V}$ALENTINE'S DAY BLESSING

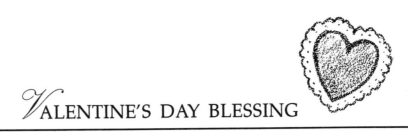

In addition to sharing cards, gifts, and other expressions of love on the feast day of St. Valentine, celebrate this day with a simple blessing.

~CALL TO WORSHIP~

Leader: God is love!

All: **And we who abide in love, abide in God.**

Leader: Father, bless the love that brings people together and grows ever stronger in our hearts. May all the messages that carry the name of your holy bishop Valentine be sent in good joy and received in delight. We ask this in the name of Jesus the Lord.[32]

All: Amen.

~WORD SERVICE~

Read one or more of the following:

John 3:16	John 15:9-14
Romans 5:8	Romans 8:35-39
1 Corinthians 13 1	John 3:1

The life of St. Valentine might be read from a biography of the saints and then discussed.

~INTERCESSIONS~

Leader: For God's love which nurtures the heart.

All: **God's love is everlasting.**

Leader: For the love of parents who helped us to love.

All: **God's love is everlasting.**

Leader: For love which brings us peace and hope.

All: **God's love is everlasting.**

Other intentions may be added by those present.

~BLESSING PRAYER~

Leader: May the peace of God which is beyond all understanding keep our hearts and minds in the knowledge and love of God and of his Son, our Lord Jesus Christ.

All: **Amen.**

Exchange an expression of peace.

$\mathscr{L}$ENTEN MEAL BLESSING

In addition to parish Lenten services, families and groups may wish to observe Lent at the table with an atmosphere of prayer and renewal. Perhaps once or twice during Lent families and friends may join together for such a service.

Prepare the table with candles and simple Lenten foods in imitation of the Seder table at Passover time: salad, hard-boiled eggs, bread and drink.

~CALL TO WORSHIP~

To symbolize God's presence, the hostess lights the candles while saying:

> Blest be the Lord, the God of creation,
> who alone does wondrous deeds.

All: **Blest be God's glorious name forever;
may the whole earth be filled with God's glory.**

The host lifts his drink-filled cup and says:

> Blest be the Lord day by day.
> Our Savior bears our burdens and is our salvation.

All: **Our help is from the Lord
who made heaven and earth.**

All drink from their cups.

~WORD SERVICE~

Reader: Deuteronomy 26:17-19
            Mark 12:28-34
            (or another reading)

The host passes around the salad, eggs, bread, and drink. Conversation may be directed to topics of Lenten renewal or to everyday opportunities for Christian witness.

~INTERCESSIONS~

Reader: God our Father, you have gathered us around this table.
            Let your word shake us out of our easy ways
            that we may repent and take positive steps in our witness to you.
            That Lent may bring a return to the covenant
            in which we love God and our neighbor as Jesus teaches,
            we pray to the Lord.

All: **Lord, renew the face of the earth.**

Reader: That Lent may be a time for truth, justice and peace in the decisions of state, national, and world governments, we pray to the Lord.

All: **Lord, renew the face of the earth.**

Reader: That Lent may be a time for positive efforts toward renewal of our covenant promises to love, we pray to the Lord.

All: **Lord, renew the face of the earth.**

Reader: That Lent may provide each family with time to strengthen bonds of love and communication, we pray to the Lord.

All: **Lord, renew the face of the earth.**

Reader: That Lent's prayers and sacrifices may bring relief to those suffering from any need, we pray to the Lord.

All: **Lord, renew the face of the earth.**

Other personal intentions may be added.

Leader: These are our prayers.

We join to them our promise to live Jesus' way of love.
We seal this prayer and promise with this last cup.
All drink. Then join in praying the Lord's Prayer.

When the meal is completed, the leader prays the blessing: [33]

Leader: The Father of mercies has given us an example of unselfish love
in the sufferings of his only Son.
Through your service of God and neighbor
may you receive his countless blessings.

All: **Amen.**

Leader: You believe that by his dying
Christ destroyed death forever.
May he give you everlasting life.

All: **Amen.**

Leader: He humbled himself for our sakes.
May you follow his example
and share in his resurrection.

All: **Amen.**

Conclude by making the sign of the cross.

ᏚAINT PATRICK'S DAY BLESSING

St. Patrick's Day, celebrated on March 17, is an occasion to celebrate the patron saint of people of Irish heritage as well as the great faith and missionary spirit of the saint.

~CALL TO PRAYER~

Leader: May God be blessed in the saints.

All: **And praised in their holy lives.**

Leader: Let us pray.
              Lord God,
              We rejoice in the great bishop Patrick
              who boldly proclaimed the good news
              to the Irish people.
              May we, like Patrick,
              give joyful witness in our love and service of others
              and make your kingdom known.
              We ask this through Christ, our Lord.

All: **Amen.**

~SCRIPTURE READING~

Isaiah 52:7-10	Acts 13:46-49
Acts 26:19-23	1 Corinthians 1:18-25
Matthew 28:16-20	Mark 16:15-20

A brief summary of the life of St. Patrick may be read and discussed.

~INTERCESSIONS~

Reader: Lord, for the gift of faith.

All: **We praise you.**

Reader: Lord, for those who proclaim good news.

All: **We praise you.**

Leader: Lord, for hope in your word.

All: **We praise you.**

~BLESSING PRAYER~

Leader: May the roads rise to meet you,
                 May the wind be always at your back.
                 May the sun shine warm upon your face,
                 The rains fall soft upon your fields,
                 And until we meet again,
                 May God hold you
                 in the hollow of his hand.

—Irish Blessing

All: **Amen.**

Festive food and drink may be shared by all. Irish songs may be sung or recorded Irish music can be enjoyed by all.

$\mathcal{S}$AINT JOSEPH'S DAY BLESSING

St. Joseph's Day is celebrated on March 19. The spouse of Mary and foster father of Jesus is remembered by many people, especially those of Italian heritage, who celebrate this day with festive meals and good works for the poor. It is an occasion to celebrate his love and care for Mary and Jesus and his firm faith in God.

~CALL TO PRAYER~

Leader: God, we praise you in your just ones.

All: And give you thanks for their witness.

Leader: Let us pray.
            God and Father,
            your son Jesus knew the love and care of St. Joseph
            who was good and just.
            With his example may we, your Church,
            demonstrate that same dedication to Christ,
            who lives and reigns with you,
            now and forever.

All: Amen.

~SCRIPTURE READING~

Matthew 1:18-24 or Luke 2:41-51

A short reading about the life of St. Joseph may be read. All may discuss the meaning of his life today.

~INTERCESSIONS~

Reader: That all who hear God's call may, like St. Joseph, respond with a
            generous heart.

All: Give praise to God!

Reader:	That St. Joseph, patron of those who are approaching death, may be with all who are journeying toward the heavenly kingdom.
All:	**Give praise to God!**
Reader:	That St. Joseph, patron of the church, may show us how to love Christ and bring him to others.
All:	**Give praise to God!**

~BLESSING PRAYER~

Leader:	Heavenly Father, from the family of your servant David you raised up Joseph to be the guardian of your incarnate Son and spouse of his virgin mother. Give us the grace to imitate his uprightness of life and his obedience to your commands, through Jesus Christ our Lord.[34]
All:	**Amen.**

All may enjoy a special dessert. A monetary contribution or clothing may be donated to a charity or organization that aids the homeless or neglected children.

PALM SUNDAY BLESSING

After participating in Sunday eucharist, all gather together in the home. The blessed palms that have been brought home can be braided or woven while fresh.

~GATHERING PRAYER~

Leader: We pray.
            Gracious God,
            hear our prayer
            as we turn to you in faith.
            As we acclaim Christ as Messiah and King,
            may our praises and the branches we bear,
            ever remind us that Jesus is the Lord
            of all our days and forever.

All: Amen.

~SCRIPTURE READING~

Matthew 21:1-11 (Year A)   Mark 11:1-10 (Year B)

John 12:12-16 (Year B)   Luke 19:28-40 (Year C)

All may discuss the liturgy celebrated at church earlier and the meaning of the Holy Week days that lie ahead.

~PLACEMENT OF PALMS~

Leader: We give thanks for these fresh palms (branches) which remind us of the joyful entry of Jesus into Jerusalem. As they lose their freshness we know that they will be used to make the ashes for a new penitential season. They remind us of the cycle of life and death and Jesus who has conquered sin and death so that we might have eternal life. Help us, Lord, to keep these days of remembrance and to rejoice in Easter life.

The palms are placed with the family cross or crucifix, or placed in the various rooms of the home.

~CLOSING PRAYER~

Leader: God,
     your Son Jesus Christ lived our humanity
     and redeemed us through his suffering
     and death on the cross.
     May we follow him with a lively faith,
     bear our sufferings with courage,
     and come to share in his eternal life.
     We ask this through Christ our Lord.

All: **Amen.**

*H*OLY THURSDAY MEAL BLESSING

At sundown Lent comes to a close and we begin the paschal triduum. Some of the traditional Passover foods (lamb, unleavened bread, bitter herbs, applesauce mixed with nuts) may be served at the meal. A candle is lit as all gather at the table.

~GATHERING PRAYER~

Leader: Let us pray. *(Pause for silent prayer.)*
           God our Father,
           we pause from the rush of life
           to recall that this day your son Jesus
           gave himself to us through the sign of a meal.
           As we share this supper may we remember
           his life given for us and his command to do this in his memory.
           Help us to love the eucharist we celebrate with our brothers and sisters,
           and to make real in our lives the great love of your Son.
           We pray this through Christ, our Lord.

All: **Amen.**

~SCRIPTURE READING~

Exodus 12:1-8,11-14

1 Corinthians 11:23-26

John 13:1-15

The meal is shared. During the meal one of the family members asks the question:

Why are these days different from others?

Another family member or guest explains the Jewish Passover, as well as the significance of the "three days" and the joy and faith celebrated at Easter.

~SACRAMENTAL GESTURE~

After the meal, the leader washes the hands of all who have dined. At the end, the leader's hands are washed by another family member. The leader prays:

> Jesus, you gave us an example of humble service by washing feet. We wash hands that have shared the meal as we remember you. May these hands reach out in service, ready to lift up and support, to love and to care. May these clean hands remind us of our desire to follow you with a clean heart. We pray this through Christ our Lord.

All: **Amen.**

If the family is unable to participate in the Mass of the Lord's Supper, they may be able to join the washing and praying later in the evening at the parish church.

*G*OOD FRIDAY MEAL BLESSING

The family gathers either at noontime (if possible) or in the evening to share a simple meal. The cross is placed in the center of the table.

~GATHERING PRAYER~

Leader: We adore you, Christ, and we praise you.

All: **Because by your holy cross you have redeemed the world.**

Leader: We pray.
God of love,
your Son Jesus shed his blood for us on the cross
and saved us from sin and eternal death.
In your great mercy, help us to shed anything that does not
unite us to you. Help us to understand the life of Jesus,
given for us, so that we may follow him in freedom.
Grant this through Christ our Lord.

All: **Amen.**

~SCRIPTURE READING~

Philippians 2:6-11

Hebrews 4:14-16; 5:7-9

John 3:13-17

~SACRAMENTAL GESTURE~

Some of the unleavened bread from yesterday's meal or other bread is broken and passed to each person. The leader prays:

As Jesus was broken for us, we give thanks and remember his great act of love. Jesus' suffering and dying saved us from sin and has given us the freedom to live in holiness. May all who suffer today be united to Jesus in his suffering and find hope and strength. Help each of us to know how to face our own trials and pain and to offer them in union with Jesus' saving death and resurrection. We pray this in Jesus' name.

All: **Amen.**

The cross may be passed to each person who reverences it. All share in the meal. A spirit of quiet and reflection is encouraged in the home, especially during the hours when we recall Christ's death on the cross. Meditative music may also aid a spirit of contemplation in the home. If possible, all participate in the liturgy of Good Friday at church.

$\mathscr{B}$LESSING OF A FAMILY EASTER CANDLE

Decorate a large candle and place it in the center of the table. Surround it with flowers. When all have gathered for Easter dinner, light the candle and make the sign of the cross.

~CALL TO WORSHIP~

Leader: Christ our Light!

All: **Thanks be to God.**

Leader: Blessed are you God, Father of all nations. You are the God of light, and in you there is no darkness. As we gather to rejoice in the risen life of your Son Jesus may our home, and those of our brothers and sisters, be bright with laughter and warm with love. We ask this in Jesus' name.

All: **Amen.**

~WORD SERVICE~

Read one of the following passages from scripture:

Luke 24:1-6	Matthew 28:1-7
Mark 16:1-8	John 20:19-23

~INTERCESSIONS~

Ask another family member to read the following prayers, pausing after each line for all to respond:

He is truly risen!

Reader: Christ our Lord has been raised. . . .
Death no longer has hold over him. . . .
He lives a new life. . . .
Alleluia, alleluia. . . .
Praise to you, Lord of Life. . . .
Peace be to you. . . .

~BLESSING OF THE CANDLE~

Leader: May the light of Christ, rising in glory,
dispel the darkness of our hearts and minds.
Heavenly Father,
accept this Easter candle,
a flame divided but undimmed,
a pillar of fire that glows to the honor of God.
Let it mingle with the lights of heaven
and continue bravely burning
to dispel the darkness of this night!
May the morning Star which never sets find this flame still burning:
Christ, that Morning Star, who came back from the dead,
and shed his peaceful light on all humanity,
your Son who lives and reigns forever and ever.[35]

All: **Amen.**

Continue lighting the candle at meals during the fifty-day period of rejoicing. On Ascension Thursday, the leader prays:

Leader: God our Father,
make us joyful in the ascension of your Son Jesus Christ.
May we follow him into the new creation,
for his ascension is our glory and our hope.
We ask this through our Lord Jesus Christ, your Son.[36]

All: **Amen.**

On Pentecost, the leader prays:

Leader: Father in heaven,
           fifty days have celebrated the fullness
           of the mystery of your revealed love.
           See your people gathered in prayer,
           open to receive the Spirit's flame.
           May it come to rest in our hearts
           and disperse the divisions of word and tongue.
           With one voice and one song
           may we praise your name in joy and thanksgiving.
           Grant this through Christ our Lord.[37]

All: **Amen.**

ℬLESSING OF EASTER FOODS

If the family is unable to go to the parish church where there is the blessing of Easter foods, the family may celebrate this blessing at home on Holy Saturday.

The Easter feast concluded the Lenten fast and the foods that were to be shared in the feast were blessed with joy and gratitude. The original foods blessed were those prescribed for the Passover meal of the Old Testament: lamb, bread, wine, bitter herbs. Other foods have since been added which "Christianize" the blessing.

~CALL TO WORSHIP~

All join in making the sign of the cross.

Leader: The Lord has freed us from our sins by his own blood.

All: **To God be glory and power forever and ever.**

Leader: Let us pray.
           Father, you give us food to share that we might be nourished and
           strengthened. Above all you have given us your Son Jesus who
           gave his life and continues to give his life as food for many. May

our gratitude for this food give you praise, through Jesus, the
Bread of Life.

All: **Amen.**

~WORD SERVICE~

One of the family members may read:

Exodus 12:1-8,11-14   Deuteronomy 8:7-19

Joel 2:21-24, 26-27   John 6:1-13

~INTERCESSIONS~

Reader: God is the giver of all good things, of every blessing. He lovingly
provides us with what we need. That the Lord may bless us with
daily bread, we pray.

All: **Father, we thank you.**

Reader: For those who hunger, that we may share with them what has been
given to us, we pray.

All: **Father, we thank you.**

Reader: For all who work with the soil, that they may have a fruitful season,
we pray.

All: **Father, we thank you.**

Reader: We mention now the needs in our own hearts . . . *(family members
may add their personal intentions).*

Reader: Let us pray for our daily bread as Jesus taught us.

All pray the Our Father.

~BLESSING PRAYER~

Leader *(with hands extended over the food):*

Lord, bless this food, created by you, that it may be a means of nourishment and festivity for us as we rejoice over the Easter victory of

your Son. May each of us who partake of these foods be renewed in body and spirit, through Jesus our Paschal Lamb, who lives and rules forever and ever.

All: **Amen.**

The food may be sprinkled with holy water. The leader may say a prayer of blessing over individual foods, following the traditional practice:

~ Blessing of the Paschal Lamb and Other Meats ~

Leader: Father of all goodness, we bless you for this lamb and these meat products. You commanded our ancestors in the faith to prepare a lamb on Passover night. May these meats prepared for our celebration in honor of the Passover of your Son from death to life remind us of the true Paschal Lamb by whose blood we are saved. May we enjoy these foods and obtain your blessing through the power of the cross and the resurrection of your Son. This we ask through him, our Risen Lord.

All: **Amen.**

~ Blessing of Bread ~

Leader: Father Almighty, may your blessing be upon this bread and all who partake of it. As with the many grains of wheat which have combined to form this loaf, may we be made one through the sharing of this food. We ask this through the risen Christ, the bread of life, the bread from heaven, who fulfills every hunger forever and ever.

All: **Amen.**

~ Blessing of Eggs ~

Leader: Heavenly Father, let your blessing be upon these eggs. In them we see a sign of your Son rising to new life from the tomb. May we share them in thankful celebration of the resurrection of your Son Jesus, who lives with you forever and ever.

All: **Amen.**

~ Blessing of Children's Easter Baskets ~

Leader: Loving Father, in joy we thank you for the Easter baskets which (*name the children*) ask your blessing upon. May they enjoy these Easter eggs and candy and all that these baskets contain as they celebrate the resurrection of Jesus, your Son and our Brother. May we always appreciate the gifts we receive and the joy you give us in sharing them through Christ our risen Lord.

All: **Amen.**

All may join in singing an Easter hymn.

EARTH DAY BLESSING

Earth Day, begun in 1970, is usually celebrated on April 22. It is an occasion to give thanks for the many blessings of creation and to pray for the wisdom to conserve earth's goodness. The prayer may take place in the family yard, at a park, or near water.

~CALL TO PRAYER~

Leader: All creation bless the Lord.

All: **And give praise to God.**

Leader: Let us pray.
God of heaven and earth,
we praise you for mother earth,
which you have wonderfully made and given to us.
Help us to always appreciate this great gift
and make us responsible stewards of this richness.
May we give honor to you by honoring earth's splendor
which you share with us and which someday we will return to you.
We make our prayer in Christ, the first-born of all creation,
now and forever.

All: **Amen.**

~SCRIPTURE READING~

Genesis 1:1—2:2
Psalm 148
Colossians 1:15-20

All may discuss how each of us is called to care for the world of nature and how we preserve and sustain God's creation.

~INTERCESSIONS~

Reader: For trees, plants, and flowers.

All: We give thanks!

Reader: For the air we breathe, for wind, and rain.

All: We give thanks!

Reader: For water, lakes, and streams.

All: We give thanks!

Reader: For the soil, for insects, and all creatures.

All: We give thanks!

(Other intercessions may be added)

~BLESSING PRAYER~

Leader: Lord,
            we rejoice that you are our Creator.
            As we bless you for all of creation,
            help us to be co-creators with you
            in caring for the gift of the earth.
            Continue to bless us with the fruit of your creation.

All: Amen.

A backyard barbecue or a picnic in a park or at the beach can be enjoyed by all. A contribution can be made to support an environmental cause. Trees, plants, and flowers can be planted in honor of Earth Day. Households can join together to clean up a littered area.

OTHER'S DAY BLESSING

Each year, on the second Sunday in May, we honor mothers with a special day dedicated to them. The following blessing may take place at the family dinner on that day.

~GATHERING PRAYER~

Leader: We pray *(pause for silence)* . . .
God,
who made Eve the mother of all the living,
and chose Mary to be the mother of your Son,
we bless you for our mother, *(name).*
Bless her with grace and peace all her days.
May she rejoice always in your love.
We ask this through Christ our Lord.

All: **Amen.**

~SCRIPTURE READING~

Sirach 3:2-6   Exodus 20:12
Psalm 71   Psalm 139
John 19:25-27

~INTERCESSIONS~

Reader: For mothers, grandmothers, godmothers, mothers-to-be, and all who are like a mother to us.

All: **Lord, we pray.**

Reader: For children who love their mothers and honor them.

All: **Lord, we pray.**

Reader: For fulfilling and happy lives for mothers.

All: **Lord, we pray.**

~BLESSING GESTURE~

All may extend their hands over the mother as the leader prays:

> Loving God, who is Father and Mother to us,
> we pray for *(name)* and for all who rejoice in motherhood.
> We thank you for her life and for her giving life to us.
> We bless you for her gentleness, love, and dedication.
> Bless her with joy and love all her days. May she,
> like all the holy women and Mary, the mother of Jesus,
> find joy in God our Savior.
> We pray this through Christ, our Lord.

All: **Amen.**

All share in the meal together. Family members may share gifts, flowers, and cards with their mother.

FATHER'S DAY BLESSING

We honor fathers in a special way on the third Sunday in June. This blessing may take place at the family dinner that day.

~GATHERING PRAYER~

Leader: We pray. *(Pause for silence.)*
God,
your Son Jesus Christ taught us to call you father
and you always show your fatherly care for us.
Bless our father, *(name)*. May he always be a
good caregiver and provider.
Give him many days and peace in his heart.
We ask this through Christ our Lord.

All: **Amen.**

~SCRIPTURE READING~

Exodus 20:12
Sirach 3:2-6, 12-14
Luke 10:21-22

~INTERCESSIONS~

Reader: For fathers, grandfathers, godfathers, fathers-to-be, and all who are
            like a father to us.

All: **Lord, we pray.**

Reader: For children who love their fathers and honor them.

All: **Lord, we pray.**

Reader: For fulfilling and happy lives for fathers.

All: **Lord, we pray.**

~BLESSING GESTURE~

All may extend their hands over the father as the leader prays:

Loving God, whom we also call Father, we pray for *(name)*
who is father to us. We thank you for his wisdom and care
for us. We bless you for his strength and patience.
Bless him withpeace and joy as we honor him all the days of his life.
May he, like the men in the scriptures and Joseph, father of
Jesus, be just and true. We ask this through Christ our Lord.

All: **Amen.**

*All share in the meal together. Family members may share a special dessert, a walk
together, and cards with their father.*

$\mathscr{L}$ABOR DAY BLESSING

Labor Day not only marks the conclusion of the summer, but also celebrates the goodness of work and the blessings of labor.

~CALL TO WORSHIP~

Leader: May the goodness of the Lord be upon us.

All: **And give success to the work of our hands (Ps 89:17).**

Leader: Let us pray.
God our Father,
by the labor of men and women you govern and guide to perfection the work of creation.
Hear the prayers of your people
and give all people work that enhances their human dignity
and draws them closer to each other
in the service of their brothers and sisters.
We ask this in Jesus' name.[38]

All: **Amen.**

~WORD SERVICE~

Read one or more of the following scripture passages:

Genesis 2:4-9,15	John 4:34-38
2 Thessalonians 3:6-12,16	Amos 9:11-15
Genesis 1:1—2:4	Luke 5:1-11

~INTERCESSIONS~

Leader: For the labor of workers.

All: **We bless you, Lord.**

Leader: For the dignity of human work.

All: **We bless you, Lord.**

Leader: For the right to work.

All: **We bless you, Lord.**

Assemble and bless a variety of tools and work equipment.

~BLESSING PRAYER~

Leader: Almighty God, your son Jesus Christ dignified our labor by sharing our toil. Bless these instruments of labor and be with your people who use them. Make those who carry on the industries and commerce of this land responsive to your will; and to all of us, give pride in what we do and a just return for our labor. Through your Son, Jesus Christ our Lord.[39]

All: **Amen.**

$\mathscr{G}$RANDPARENT'S DAY BLESSING

Since 1979, a yearly remembrance of grandparents, usually on the first Sunday in September following Labor Day, has gained in popularity as a day to especially remember our beloved grandparents. This blessing can take place where they live or at the home of their children. A festive dinner prepared for them can form part of the celebration.

~GATHERING PRAYER~

Leader: We pray. *(Pause for silence).*
            Lord, our God,
            we praise you for *(names of grandparents present)*
            who bless us with life, love, and heritage.
            Be with them, guard and sustain them all their days
            and grant them abundant peace and joy.
            We pray this in Jesus' name.

All: **Amen.**

~SCRIPTURE READING~

Sirach 44:1,10-15
Matthew 13:16-17

~INTERCESSIONS~

Reader: For our grandparents who passed on to us the gift of life.

All: **We give thanks!**

Reader: For wisdom, age, and grace.

All: **We give thanks!**

Reader: For the heritage of faith.

All: **We give thanks!**

~BLESSING GESTURE~

All may extend their hands over the grandparent(s) as the leader prays:

Bless, Lord, our grandparents *(names)*.
Give them the joy of your presence
and fill their days with peace. May they
always know our love and gratefulness. May
they know they are the real treasures of our family.
We pray this through Christ our Lord.

All: **Amen.**

All share a festive dinner. Family members may share gifts, flowers, and cards with grandparent(s). Family photo albums and stories may be shared and enjoyed.

ALL SAINTS' DAY BLESSING

On the feast of All Saints (or on a saint's particular feast) we bless the Lord for the lives of those who witnessed him and ask that we might reflect their example. Highlights of the life of a particular saint being remembered may be shared before the blessing celebration or following the reading of the word.

~CALL TO WORSHIP~

Leader: Let us rejoice in the Lord!

All: And bless God in his saints.

Leader: Let us pray.
            God our Father,
            source of all holiness,
            the work of your hands is manifest in your saints,
            the beauty of your truth is reflected in their faith.
            May we who aspire to have part in their joy
            be filled with the Spirit that blessed their lives,
            so that having shared their faith on earth
            we may also know their peace in your kingdom.
            Grant this through Christ our Lord.[40]

All: Amen.

~WORD SERVICE~

Read one of the following scripture passages:

            Matthew 5:1-12
            1 John 3:1-3
            Revelation 7:2-4, 9-14

~INTERCESSIONS~

Reader: Holy Mary, mother of God,

All: Pray for us.

Reader: St. John the Baptist,

All: **Pray for us.**

Reader: St. Joseph,

All: **Pray for us.**

Reader: Saint Peter and Saint Paul,

All: **Pray for us.**

Reader: *(Add the names of other saints, especially the patrons of the children, the church or the locality. Pause for the response after each name.)*

The litany concludes:

Reader: All you saints of God,

All: **Pray for us.**[41]

The leader may impose hands upon each person.

Leader: Almighty God, you have surrounded us with a great cloud of witnesses. Grant that we, encouraged by the good example of your saints (*your servant, name*) may persevere in running the race that is set before us, until at last we may attain to your eternal joy; through Jesus Christ, the pioneer and perfector of our faith, who lives and reigns with you and the Holy Spirit, one God, forever and ever.[42]

All: **Amen.**

Share a special dessert or treat, if desired.

$\mathscr{B}$LESSING UPON VISITING A GRAVE

The church has traditionally remembered the deceased, especially during the month of November. The Feast of All Souls recalls the faithful departed and invites us to remember all who have fallen asleep in Christ.

~CALL TO WORSHIP~

Leader: Jesus died and rose again.

All: **The Father will gather those who have fallen asleep in Christ.**

~or~

Leader: Give them eternal rest, O Lord.

All: **And may your light shine on them forever.**

Leader: Let us pray. (*Pause for silent prayer.*)
Merciful Father,
hear our prayers and console us.
As we renew our faith in your Son,
whom you raised from the dead,
strengthen our hope that all our departed brothers and sisters
will share in his resurrection
who lives and reigns with you and the Holy Spirit,
one God, forever and ever.[43]

All: **Amen.**

~WORD SERVICE~

Select one of the following:

Wisdom 3:1-9	Matthew 25:31-46
Isaiah 25:6,7-9	John 11:17-27
Romans 6:3-9	1 Corinthians 15:20-24, 25-28

~INTERCESSIONS~

Reader: Jesus Christ is the first-born from the dead.

All: Glory to him!

Reader: We believe we shall become like him.

All: Glory to him!

Reader: Our hope is in the Lord.

All: Glory to him!

All who have gathered may kneel at the graveside. The leader may bless those present, and the grave with holy water as a reminder of our baptismal commitment to enter into the death and resurrection of Christ.

~BLESSING PRAYER~

Leader: Almighty God, we remember before you today your faithful ser-
           vant (*name*); and we pray that, having opened to him (her) the gates
           of larger life, you will receive him (her) more and more into your
           joyful service, that, with all who have faithfully served you in the
           past, he (she) may share in the eternal victory of Jesus Christ our
           Lord; who lives and reigns with you, in the unity of the Holy Spirit,
           one God, forever and ever.[44]

All: Amen.

Place flowers at the grave, if desired, as a reminder of the life and love of the deceased person.

Occasional Blessings

$\mathscr{B}$LESSING OF THE HOME

This blessing may take place when a family moves into a new home or yearly as a rededication. Gather in the living room of the home.

~CALL TO WORSHIP~

Leader: Peace to this house.

All: **And to all who live here.**

Leader: Let us pray.
Almighty and everlasting God, grant to this home the grace of your presence, that you may be known to be the inhabitant of this dwelling, and the defender of this household. Through Jesus Christ our Lord, who with you and the Holy Spirit lives and reigns forever and ever.[45]

All: **Amen.**

~WORD SERVICE~

One of the family members reads a passage from the family Bible.

Genesis 18:1-8	Luke 10:38-42
Matthew 10:1, 5-16	Romans 12:9-16

~INTERCESSIONS~

Reader: May the Lord bless us abundantly in his love.

All: **Blessed be God.**

Reader: May the Lord grant us the spirit of peace.

All: **Blessed be God.**

Reader: May we welcome all visitors here as Christ.

All: **Blessed be God.**

~BLESSING PRAYER~

The leader may sprinkle the house with holy water. An image of Christ or the holy family may be prominently placed.

Leader: Visit, blessed Lord, this home with the gladness of your presence. Bless all who live here with the gift of your love; and grant that we may manifest your love (to each other and) to all whose lives we touch. May we grow in grace and in the knowledge and love of you; guide, comfort, and strengthen us. Preserve us in peace, Jesus Christ, now and forever.[46]

All: **Amen.**

~or~

Bless the rooms individually.

~ At the Entrance ~

Leader: Sovereign Lord, you are Alpha and Omega, the beginning and the end. Send your servants out from this place on many errands, be their constant companion on the way, and welcome them upon their return, so that coming and going they may be sustained by your presence. Through Christ our Lord.[47]

All: **Amen.**

~ In the Living Room or Family Room ~

Leader: Bless this living room that here we may find our bonds of friendship joyfully renewed and deepened after days of study and work, play and growth. May your peace always stay in this room, making it a place where we can each grow into better friends with you and with one another. Through Christ our Lord.[48]

All: **Amen.**

~ In the Kitchen ~

Leader: Lord our God, you supply every need of ours according to your great riches. Bless the hands that work in this place, and give us grateful hearts for daily bread. Through Christ our Lord.[49]

All: Amen.

~ *In the Dining Room or Area* ~

Leader: Blessed are you, Lord, King of the Universe, for you give us food and drink to sustain our lives. Make us grateful for all your mercies, and mindful of the needs of others. Through Jesus Christ our Lord.[50]

All: **Amen.**

~ *In a Bedroom* ~

Leader: God of life and love, the true rest of your people sanctify our hours of rest and refreshment, our sleeping and waking. Grant that strengthened by the indwelling of the Holy Spirit, we may rise to serve you all the days of our life. Through Jesus Christ our Lord.[51]

All: **Amen.**

~ *In a Child's Room* ~

Leader: Heavenly Father, your Son our Savior took children in his arms and blessed them. Embrace the child whose room this is with your unfailing love. Protect him (her) from all danger, and bring him (her) in safety to each new day, until he (she) greets with joy the great day of your kingdom. Through Jesus Christ our Lord.[52]

All: **Amen.**

~ *In a Guest Room* ~

Leader: Loving God, you have taught us to welcome one another as Christ welcomed us. Bless those who from time to time share the hospitality of this home. May your protective care shield them, the love of Jesus preserve them from all evil, and the guidance of your Holy Spirit keep them in the way that leads to eternal life. Through Jesus Christ our Lord.[53]

All: **Amen.**

~ In a Bathroom ~

Leader: Father, you gave us bodies that we might be the living body of Christ on earth. Grant a blessing which fills this room, so that out of love for you we may always care for our bodies as the living temples of your Holy Spirit. Through Christ our Lord.[54]

All: **Amen.**

~ Recreation Area or Backyard ~

Leader: Father, you richly shared your precious gift of life with us. Bless this place of rest and leisure time, that in our play and recreation, we may find refreshment and fulfillment for our busy lives.Through Christ our Lord.[55]

All: **Amen.**

~ In a Workroom or Workshop ~

Leader: God, your blessed Son worked with his hands in the carpenter shop in Nazareth. Be present, we pray, with those who work in this place, that laboring as workers together with you, they may share the joy of your creation. Through Christ our Lord.[56]

All: **Amen.**

Exchange an embrace or a gesture of love. All may join in a song of praise.

$\mathscr{B}$LESSING OF A VEHICLE

Celebrate the following blessing upon the purchase of a car or other vehicle (recreational or practical), or as a yearly blessing of vehicles in the parish. It may also be used prior to vacation travel.

~CALL TO WORSHIP~

Leader: The Lord be with you.

All: And also with you.

Leader: Let us pray.
            Lord God, listen to our prayers as we ask your blessing upon this car (truck, boat, these vehicles). You have graciously provided for our needs in the past, so now we ask your blessing upon this vehicle (these vehicles) and our use of it (them). May all our travels and enjoyments lead us to you, our lasting joy. Through Christ our Lord.

All: Amen.

~WORD SERVICE~

Select from the following:
            Tobit 5:4-9
            Mark 6:30-32 or Mark 6:45-52 (blessing of a boat)
            John 14:5-7

~INTERCESSIONS~

Reader: Father, bless all who use this car (truck, boat, these vehicles). May they be conscious of their responsibility toward others.

All: Lord, hear us.

Reader: Help us to avoid all danger and accident by our carefulness.

All: Lord, hear us.

Reader: Protect us from harm and bring us back home in peace and joy.

All: Lord, hear us.

~BLESSING PRAYER~

Leader: Lord God, you are the maker of every good gift. You have seen fit to share with us the wonders of creation. We ask you now to bless this vehicle (these vehicles) and all who use it (them). May all who benefit by it (them) in their travels be responsible, always considerate and helpful to others. We make this prayer in Jesus' name.

All: **Amen.**

Bless the vehicle(s) with holy water, if desired. Families may want to place an image of Christ in their vehicle as a sign of dedication and a reminder of the Lord's presence and blessing.

$\mathcal{B}$LESSING BEFORE TRAVEL

Gather before a journey to invoke God's blessing upon the journey.

~CALL TO WORSHIP~

Leader: May the Lord be with us in our travels.

All: **And guide us in safety and joy.**

Leader: Let us pray.

Hear us, Lord, as we ask you to accompany us. May our journey help us to appreciate your creation and refresh us in body and spirit. May we reach our destination safely and return home in peace and joy. We ask this through Christ our Lord.

All: **Amen.**

~WORD SERVICE~

Select from the following:

Genesis 28:10-15	Tobit 5:4-7
Luke 1:39-56	Luke 3:1-6
Luke 10:25-37	

~INTERCESSIONS~

Reader: Let us ask God's blessing for each of us on our travels
        and for all who are traveling.
        That you may safely guide us to our destination,
        we pray to the Lord.

All: **Lord, be with us.**

Reader: That your peace and protection may accompany us
        and all who travel today, we pray to the Lord.

All: **Lord, be with us.**

Reader: That we may always be considerate of others
        and mindful of safety, we pray to the Lord.

All: **Lord, be with us.**

Add other prayers, if desired. Conclude with the Lord's Prayer.

~BLESSING PRAYER~

The leader then prays over all:

Leader: May the Lord watch over us and guide us on our journey. May his
saints and angels be with us to protect us on our way. May no harm
come to us and may we reach our destination in peace and safety.
And may we return safely with the Lord who is our companion and
who is present to us always and everywhere.

All: **Amen.**

~or~

Leader: God, we marvel at your providence which has given your holy
angels care over us. You sent the archangel Raphael to accompany
Tobias on his journey. Grant that he may also watch over us in our
travels. May he, who stands before your throne, present our prayers
for your blessing, that we may be safe under his protection and
happy in his company for all eternity. We ask this through Christ
our Lord.

All: **Amen.**

Leader: Let us go forth in peace and joy.

All: **Thanks be to God.**

$\mathscr{B}$LESSING AT THE BEGINNING AND CONCLUSION OF A PREGNANCY

This prayer may be celebrated at the announcement of pregnancy as well as just before childbirth, for a safe and happy delivery of a new child.

~CALL TO PRAYER~

Leader: The Lord be with you.

All: **And also with you.**

Leader: Let us pray.

Loving God, look with love upon *(name the mother)* and her child. Bless her husband, *(name)*, and guide them. May their child grow in wisdom, age and grace in your presence and before all people.
We praise you, Father, and make this our prayer through Jesus your Son.

All: **Amen.**

~WORD SERVICE~

A family member or friend may choose one of the following:

Mark 9:35-37
Mark 10:13-16
Luke 1:39-45 (or 39-56)

~INTERCESSIONS~

Reader: Blessed are you, Lord God. You have blessed the union of *(name the parents)*.

All: **Amen.**

Reader: Blessed are you, Lord God. May this time of pregnancy be for *(name the parents)* months of drawing closer to you and to each other.

All: **Amen.**

Reader: Blessed are you, Lord God. May *(name the parents)* experience of birth be full of awe and wonder and the joy of sharing in your creation.[57]

All: **Amen.**

~BLESSING PRAYER~

Leader: Lord and giver of life, receive our prayer for *(name the mother)*, and for the child she has conceived (is about to deliver), that she and her husband, *(name)*, may happily come to the time of birth and rejoice in your loving gift of life. We ask this through our Lord Jesus Christ, a child born for us and given to us as Redeemer, now and forever.

All: **Amen.**

The parents may wish to announce the names they have chosen for either a boy or a girl and the significance of those names.

Embrace the expectant parents. Gifts for the new child may be given.

ℬLESSING OF A SICK PERSON

Share this blessing with someone who is sick.

~CALL TO WORSHIP~

Leader: The Lord has truly borne our sufferings.

All: **He has carried all our sorrows.**

Leader: Let us pray.
Lord our God, accept the fervent prayers of your people; in the multitude of your mercies look with compassion upon us and all who turn to you for help; for you are gracious, lover of souls, and to you we give glory, Father, Son, and Holy Spirit, now and forever.[58]

All: **Amen.**

~WORD SERVICE~

Read one of the following passages:

> Sirach 38:8-10, 12-14   Isaiah 53:1-5, 10-11
> 2 Corinthians 4:16-18   James 5:14-16
> Luke 8:43-48   Matthew 8:14-17
> Mark 5:21-24, 35-42 (sick child)

~INTERCESSIONS~

Reader: God always answers prayers made in faith. We pray now for *(name)*, that the Lord may help him (her) in this illness. God the Father, your will for all people is health and salvation.

All: **Lord, hear our prayer.**

Reader: Holy Trinity, one God, in you we live and move and have our being.

All: **Lord, hear our prayer.**

Reader: Lord, give *(name)* the security of knowing that he (she) is always in your care.

All: **Lord, hear our prayer.**

Other petitions may be added. Conclude with the Lord's Prayer.

~BLESSING PRAYER~

The leader may lay hands upon the sick person. Others, afterward, may do the same.

Leader: *(Name)*, I lay my hands upon you in the name of the Father, and of the Son, and of the Holy Spirit, asking our Lord Jesus Christ to sustain you with his presence, to drive away all sickness of body and spirit, and to give you that victory of life and peace which will enable you to sense him both now and evermore.[59]

All: **Amen.**

~ *For a Sick Child* ~

Leader: Lord Jesus Christ, Good Shepherd of the sheep, you gather the lambs in your arms and carry them in your bosom: We commend to your loving care this child *(name)*. Relieve his (her) pain, guard him (her) from all danger, restore to him (her) your gifts of gladness and strength, and raise him (her) up to a life of service to you. Hear us, we pray, for your dear name's sake.[60]

All: **Amen.**

$\mathscr{B}$LESSING OF AN ENGAGEMENT [61]

The decision to become engaged is a significant one in the life of a man and a woman, and offers an occasion for prayer. This blessing may be celebrated by the parents of the couple during a gathering of both families and close friends.

Begin, where appropriate, with the sign of the cross.

~CALL TO WORSHIP~

Leader: Let us bless the Lord for *(name the couple)*.

All: **Praise to you, Lord Jesus Christ.**

Leader: Let us pray.
Father in heaven, your Son Jesus saw in the love man and woman have for each other the love he himself has for your church. May your love always be upon *(names)*, today, tomorrow, and each day of their lives. We ask this through Christ our Lord.

All: **Amen.**

~WORD SERVICE~

Read one of the following passages:

> Matthew 6:25-35   John 15:9-12
> 1 Corinthians 13:1-13   Philippians 2:1-4

~INTERCESSION~

Reader: Together let us bring before the Lord our needs and the needs of others.

Couple: We glorify you.

All: **We praise you.**

Reader: That Jesus may be the foundation of love for *(names)* in their future together, we pray.

Couple:	We glorify you.
All:	**We praise you.**
Reader:	That divine providence may lead them to the bond of marriage, we pray.
Couple:	We glorify you.
All:	**We praise you.**

Add other intentions, if desired. Then join in praying the Lord's Prayer.

~BLESSING PRAYER~

The parents extend their hands over their children and pray as the leader says:

> Loving Father, we thank you for leading (*names*) to each other. As they desire to someday unite themselves to each other in marriage, may you now bless their intentions and keep them always close to you and your son Jesus, whose example of love is the source of all love, human and divine. We ask this through Christ our Lord.

All:	Amen.

If there is a ring to be exchanged, the man holds the ring as it is blessed.

Leader:	Almighty and eternal God, may this ring which symbolizes the hopes of (*names*) be a sign of their love for each other and for you. May God the Father, Son, and Holy Spirit bless you always.
All:	**Amen.**
Leader:	Let us rejoice in the Lord.
All:	**His love is everlasting.**

Share expressions of peace and love.

*B*LESSING ON ONE'S BIRTHDAY

A birthday is an occasion to bless God for the gift of life and love. Share in a blessing prayer during a birthday celebration.

~CALL TO WORSHIP~

Leader: It is with special joy and happiness that we all come together today to celebrate the birthday of *(name)*. May we all give our thanks to God for *(name)* life, and pray that he (she) will always know the greatness of his gifts of love.

Let us pray.

Father of every blessing, we bless you for the life that you have given *(name)*. May he (she) always know your love and continue to grow in age and wisdom. We join our love to yours for him (her) and make this prayer in Jesus' name.

All: **Amen.**

~WORD SERVICE~

The honored person or another may read the appropriate scripture passage.

Luke 2:6-16 (child's birthday)
Luke 2:41-52 (young person's birthday)
John 15:9-17 (adult's birthday)

~INTERCESSIONS~

Leader: We are glad that the gift of love is a part of the life of *(name)*. As the years go by may we all grow in our love and trust in each other.

All: **Hear us, Lord of life.**

Leader: For the many gifts and talents you have given to *(name)*. We have been enriched by them and blessed through him (her).

All: **Hear us, Lord of life.**

Leader: For all who celebrate the gift of life. May we always reverence the wonder of your creation in and around us.

All: **Hear us, Lord of life.**

All may join in praying the Lord's Prayer.

~BLESSING PRAYER~

Leader: Living God, our times are in your hand. Look with favor, we pray, on your servant (*name*) as he (she) begins another year of life. Grant that he (she) may grow in wisdom and grace, and strengthen his her) trust in your goodness all the days of his (her) life. Through Jesus Christ our Lord.[62]

All: **Amen.**

Embrace the birthday person. Share greetings and gifts.

$\mathcal{B}$LESSING UPON RETIREMENT

This blessing is celebrated on the occasion of a retirement to wish the person well as he or she begins a new chapter in life.

~CALL TO WORSHIP~

Leader: Glorify the Lord with me.

All: **Let us praise God's name.**

Leader: Let us pray.
Lord our God, we give you thanks for your gift of time. You bless each moment of our lives and fill it with meaning and purpose. Teach us to number our days so that we may harvest a rich life and know the rewards of our labors. We make this prayer through Christ our Lord.

All: **Amen.**

~WORD SERVICE~

The retiree or another family member or friend reads God's word.

        Matthew 5:14-16
        Hebrews 6:10-12
        (or another scripture passage)

~INTERCESSIONS~

Reader: For every hour, minute, and second, Father, that we may gain wisdom of heart.

All: **You are praised.**

Reader: For the opportunity to have served you in others and to reflect your goodness in work.

All: **You are praised.**

Reader: For *(name)*, that he (she) will find new meaning in life as he (she) continues to do your will.

All: **You are praised.**

Other prayers may be added. Then join in the Lord's Prayer.

~BLESSING PRAYER~

Leader: Lord God, you have blessed us with many gifts which we seek to put at the service of your kingdom. Bless *(name)*, as he (she) looks forward to a new and sturdy growth in life. Help him (her) to know retirement not as an end but as a beginning, to know the joy of a new and gentle work made in perfect love. Give him (her) health in mind, body, and spirit so that the days to come will be a new creation, a new path. This we ask in the name of your Son, risen and living in each of us, guiding all our days.

All: **Amen.**

Embrace the retiree and offer good wishes. Gifts of gratitude may be given.

$\mathscr{B}$LESSING UPON BEGINNING A NEW JOB

Share prayers and blessing, calling upon God for guidance and wisdom upon beginning a new job.

~CALL TO WORSHIP~

Leader:　　I will bless the Lord at all times.

All:　　　I will God's praise speak forever.

Leader:　　Let us pray.

God, ever generous and caring in all our needs, we thank you and bless you for guiding us on the journey of life and lighting the path of unknown ways. May our hearts trust the way you have prepared and help us to be generous in sharing your goodness.
Through Christ our Lord.

All:　　　Amen.

~WORD SERVICE~

2 Corinthians 6:1-3
Matthew 25:14-30
(other scripture passages may be chosen as well)

~INTERCESSIONS~

Reader:　　Bless *(name)*, as he (she) begins a new job and give him (her) the grace and strength to carry it out.

All:　　　Lord, hear us.

Reader:　　Bless us, help us to support one another in our efforts and endeavors.

All:　　　Lord, hear us.

Reader:　　Bless all who begin new paths in daily work and living; guide them in your truth.

All:　　　Lord, hear us.

~BLESSING PRAYER~

Leader: Lord of heaven and earth, we give you the glory due your holy name. We call on your name to bless *(name)*, as he (she) begins a new job (position/assignment). Give him (her) the needed guidance so that his (her) efforts will be fruitful and valuable. May all our efforts build up your kingdom where you live with Jesus and the Spirit, forever and ever.

All: **Amen.**

Family and friends share in congratulating their relative or friend. A special dessert or a toast can be shared to commemorate the occasion.

𝓑LESSING ON THE BAPTISMAL ANNIVERSARY

The baptismal anniversary is an occasion to renew baptismal vows and to bless God for the grace of redemption in Christ. The person's baptismal candle may be placed in the room, along with other mementos of the baptism. The blessing celebration may also take place within the context of a meal.

~CALL TO WORSHIP~

Leader: I have called you by name, says the Lord.

All: **You are mine forever.**

Leader: Let us pray.
Gracious Lord, we bless you as we recall the day of *(name)* baptism. On this day you called him (her) to be your son (daughter) and to be one with Christ in your church. May each of us cherish the memory of our baptism as the day of new birth by water and the spirit. We make this prayer through Christ our Lord.

All: **Amen.**

Sprinkle everyone with holy water and make the sign of the cross.

~WORD SERVICE~

Choose from the following passages:

Ezekiel 36:24-28   Mark 1:9-11
John 7:37-39   Romans 6:3-5
1 Corinthians 12:12-13

~INTERCESSIONS~

Reader: Lead us by a holy life to the joys of God's kingdom, we pray.

All: Lord, hear our prayer.

Reader: Keep our family always in your love, we pray.

All: Lord, hear our prayer.

Reader: Renew the grace of our baptism in each one of us, we pray.

All: Lord, hear our prayer.[63]

Pray together the Apostles' Creed or the Nicene Creed.

~BLESSING PRAYER~

The leader lays his or her hands upon the person's head and prays:

Leader: *(Name)*, we commend you to the mercy and grace of God our almighty
            Father, of his only Son, and of the Holy Spirit. May he protect your
            path, so that walking in the light of faith, you may come to the good
            things he has promised us. Through Christ our Lord.[64]

All: Amen.

Exchange a sign of love and peace. A song may be sung by all.

$\mathscr{B}$LESSING UPON THE NEW SCHOOL YEAR[65]

Gather some symbols of summer—a swimming certificate, a tennis ball, a jar of preserves, a map of a summer trip. Place these on a table with symbols of school—textbooks, lunch boxes, ruler, pencils.

~CALL TO WORSHIP~

Leader: Summer has been a time for new adventures, for relaxing recreation and for informal learning. As we share what we have gained from this summer, let us remember that God our Father has given us minds and hearts to grow so that we can become fuller persons and thus more like his Son Jesus.

At this point, encourage some participants to share a symbol of the summer and describe what he or she learned about self and life from the activity connected with the symbol.

Leader: Thanksgiving is the most important attitude we can have toward God. We call Jesus' gift of himself to us eucharist, which means thanksgiving or, perhaps better, thanks-living. Let us remember the happenings of our summer and thank our Father for them, as we respond:

All: **Thank you, God!**

Leader: For friends we visited or who visited us, sharing their life with us, we say. . .

For vacations and gardens, for ball games and bike riding, for swimming and suntans, we say. . .

For the sun and wind and rain, for lakes and mountains and prairies, for grass and flowers and trees and blue skies, we say. . .

Add other "Thank you's," if desired.

Leader: God of all goodness, we bring before you the joys of summer. We remember that all life comes from you and that we share your life in learning and loving your creation. Thank you for the gift of life in your Son. May the coming months bring us closer to you, through Jesus, our brother and Lord.

All: **Amen.**

~WORD SERVICE~

Leader: The informal learning we shared this summer becomes more formal when school begins. Each year brings the opportunity to grow and to become richer in knowledge through new classes, teachers, books, and experiences. Each new school year permits us to make important choices about how we use or abuse time in class and in life. We can decide how to use the next nine months for growth or for waste. Listen to a reading which prompts us to seek wisdom.

Reader: Proverbs 8:32-36

Discussion may follow, depending on the age of the children.

Leader: Let us spend a few moments in silent reflection. What do we hope to gain from the coming school year? Let us also prepare to share our prayer for the coming school year.

Allow time for silent reflection and preparation for prayer.

~INTERCESSIONS~

Leader: We bring our hopes and fears about school before you, Father, knowing that you want only our growth as persons beloved by your Son Jesus.

Participants may share their prayers for the year.

Leader: Dear God, we know that your strength will be with us in the coming months. We want to make them months of growth and learning, but we sometimes get lazy and do not make the necessary effort. When this happens, remind us that with your love we can do all things. With your grace, tasks and assignments which seem to be almost impossible become possible and joyful. We know you will be with us, through your Son Jesus.

All: **Amen.**

~BLESSING PRAYER~

Leader: May the Lord walk behind you and before you. May his strength be a light to you this year, and may he bless you through Jesus!

Person: Amen!

$\mathscr{B}$LESSING ON AN ANNIVERSARY

This blessing may be celebrated in conjunction with a dinner celebration or gathering celebrating a marriage, ordination, or vows.

~CALL TO WORSHIP~

Leader: Proclaim with me the greatness of the Lord.

All: **Together let us bless God's name.**

Leader: Let us pray.

(for married couple)
God our Father,
you created man and woman
to love each other
in the bond of marriage.
Bless and strengthen (*names*).
May their marriage become an
increasingly more perfect sign
of the union between Christ
and his church.
We ask this through our Lord
Christ.[66]

Let us pray.

(for clergy/religious)
Lord Jesus Christ, you
became poor for our sake, that
we might be made rich through
your poverty. Guide and sanctify, we pray, those whom you
call to follow you under the
vows (promises) of poverty,
celibacy, and obedience, that
by their prayer and service they
may enrich your church, and Jesus
by their life and worship may
glorify your name. You reign
with the Father and the Holy
Spirit, one God, now and
forever.[67]

All: **Amen.**

~WORD SERVICE~

Select from the following passages:

Marriage
Genesis 1:26-28, 31
1 Corinthians 12:31-13:8
Ephesians 5:25-33
Colossians 3:12-17
Mark 10:6-9
John 2:1-11

Orders/Vows
Isaiah 61:1-3
Acts 10:37-43
Romans 12:4-8
Matthew 20:25-28
Mark 10:17-31

~INTERCESSIONS~

Leader: For the covenant of love that you have established between us,

All: **We thank you, Lord.**

Leader: For the love of family and friends,

All: **We thank you, Lord.**

Leader: For the grace to continue serving the Lord with steadfast love,

All: **We thank you, Lord.**

~RENEWAL OF COMMITMENT~

The following renewal of promises is made separately by husband and wife:
(Name of husband or wife),
(number of years) years ago I circled your finger with this ring as a sign of unbroken love and as a promise of care and concern without end.
Today, I repeat that promise and take you again to myself as God's gift.
Place ring on spouse's finger.

We are one body and one life in Christ, come what may, now and forever.[68]
All: **Amen.**

The following renewal of promises is made by the clergy or religious, adapting where necessary:
My brothers and sisters, *(number of years)* years ago, I freely and fully gave myself to the service of Christ and of his body, the church.
Today, with gladness, I repeat the promise (vow) of poverty, celibacy, and obedience for the sake of the kingdom.
May God who began this good work in me bring it to completion.
All: **Amen.**

~BLESSING PRAYER~

For married couple:
All present may extend their
hands over the couple.
Leader:
Father, you have blessed and
sustained *(names)* in the bond
of marriage. Continue to increase their love in the joys and
sorrows of life, and help them
grow in holiness all their days.
We ask this through Christ our
Lord.

All: **Amen.**

For clergy/religious:
All present may extend their
hands over the couple.
Leader:
God our Father, guide of
humanity and ruler of creation,
look upon your servant *(name)*
who wishes to renew his (her)
offering of self to you. As the
years pass by, help him (her) to
enter more deeply into the
mystery of the church and to
dedicate himself (herself) more
generously to the good of
humanity. We ask this through
Christ our Lord.

All: **Amen.**

Pray together the Lord's Prayer. Embrace the person or persons celebrating the anniversary.

$\mathscr{B}$LESSING OF PETS

This blessing may take place after Mass or at a separate celebration, perhaps on the feast of St. Francis of Assisi which is celebrated on October 4.

Join in an opening song.

~CALL TO WORSHIP~

Leader: Bless the Lord, all you creatures of the Lord.

All: **Praise and exult God forever.**

Leader: Let us pray.
Creator God, you have made us and these pets and all living things. You are even more wonderful than the things you have made. We thank you for giving us these pets who give us joy. As you take care of us, so also we ask that we might take care of our pets who trust us to take care of them. By doing this, we share in your own love for all creation. We ask this in Jesus' name.

All: **Amen.**

~WORD SERVICE~

Select from the following scripture passages:

Genesis 1:24-31
Psalm 104:10-25
Matthew 6:26

~INTERCESSIONS~

Leader: For all your creatures that breathe and move and have life.

All: **Thank you, Lord.**

Leader: That we may love and honor the works of God's hand.

All: **Thank you, Lord.**

Leader: That each pet here may be treasured with care.

All: **Thank you, Lord.**

~BLESSING PRAYER~

Leader: Most high, almighty Lord, our Father,
               Yours are the praise, the glory, the honor, and all blessings!
               To you alone, Father, do all things belong.
               Be praised, Father, for giving us the animals, birds, and fish
                   which fill your world.
               Father, may we think of you and thank you when we play with
                   or care for our pets.
               Be praised, Father, for making us so happy to have our pets and
                   to have them to play with.
               We ask you, Father, that we may be good to our pets always, so
                   that they may be happy also.
               Help us always to take care of our pets so that they will be healthy.
               Father, your world is wonderful. May we all come into your even
                   greater world of the kingdom of heaven where we shall see even
                   greater things and where we shall all live and love forever.
               We ask this through Christ our Lord. [69]

All: **Amen.**

A concluding song may be sung and the animals sprinkled with holy water.

ℬLESSING OF A FAMILY TREASURE

This blessing may be celebrated when a family, or an individual in a family, wishes to express gratefulness and thanksgiving for something that has special religious significance, such as a Bible or a religious image.

~CALL TO PRAYER~

Leader: Let us bless the Lord.

All: Now and forever!

Leader: We pray.
God, you are the creator of all things,
and you give us the wisdom to enjoy
the goodness of your creation.
Help us to appreciate the many gifts
you give us, especially gifts that really
matter. May we be generous and learn
to value the gifts that last forever.
We pray this through Christ our Lord.

All: **Amen.**

~SCRIPTURE READING~

Colossians 1:12-20
Ephesians 3:14-19
Luke 11:5-13

All may discuss the significance of the item being blessed and our good and holy use of things.

~INTERCESSIONS~

Reading: Bless us, Lord, and the gifts you give us, we pray.

All: **Lord, hear us.**

Reader: Bless our use of your creation, we pray.

All: **Lord, hear us.**

Reader: Bless our sharing and generosity, we pray.

All: **Lord, hear us.**

All join together in praying the Lord's Prayer.

~BLESSING PRAYER~

Leader: Bless, Lord, *(name of person seeking the blessing),* and his (her) *(name the object being blessed)* which is being blessed in your name. May this treasure, which has special significance for *(name)* remind us of your unfailing goodness for each of us. Help us to treasure you in each other and to give thanks for your many blessings. We make this prayer through Jesus our Lord.

All: **Amen.**

Brief
Scriptural
Blessings

~

Blessed be you, Lord, God of tenderness and
compassion, rich in kindness and faithfulness,
who keeps us in your love forever! (Ex 34:6-7).

~

The Lord our God is a God of mercy.
Give glory to God! (Dt 4:31).

~

May the Lord bless us and keep us!
May the Lord's face shine on us and be gracious to us!
May the Lord's countenance be shown to us and give us peace!
    (Nm 6:24-26).

~

Blessed be our God from everlasting to everlasting!
And blessed be your name of glory, which surpasses all
    blessing and praise! (Neh 9:5).

~

Blessed be God!
Blessed be God's great name!
Blessed be all God's holy angels!
Blessed be God's great name forevermore!
Blessed be all God's angels forever! (Tb 11:14).

~

Blessed be the Lord, the God of Israel, who alone performs
    marvels!
Blessed forever be God's glorious name!
May the whole world be filled with God's glory! (Ps 72:18-19).

~

Blessed be you, Lord,
God of the humble and help of the oppressed!
Blessed be you, Lord,
support of the weak and refuge of the forsaken!
Blessed be you, Lord,
savior of the despairing —
to you be eternal glory! (Jdt 9:11).

~

Blessed be you, Father, Lord of heaven and earth!
You hide your mystery from the learned and clever,
but you reveal it to mere children.
Yes, Father, for such is your gracious will (Mt 11:25-26).

~

May you be blessed, Lord Jesus,
who died for our sins
and rose again for our life!
To you be glory forever! (Rom 4:25).

~

Blessed be the God of hope and consolation!
May God help us all to be tolerant with one another,
following the example of Jesus Christ!
So that, united in mind and voice, we may give glory
to the God and Father of our Lord Jesus Christ! (Rom 15:5-6).

~

May the God of hope fill us
with every joy and with peace, in the faith!
May hope overflow in us
through the power of the Holy Spirit (Rom 16:25, 27).

~

~

To the Father, who can give us the strength
to live according to the gospel and the message of Jesus Christ,
to God who alone is wise,
through Jesus Christ, be glory and power forever!
May God our Father strengthen us until the last day
so that we may be without blame
on the Day of our Lord Jesus Christ!
God, who calls us to union
with his Son Jesus, our Lord, is faithful.
To God be glory forever! (1 Cor 1:8-9).

~

Let us give thanks to God, who gives us victory
through our Lord Jesus Christ! (1 Cor 15:57).

~

Maranatha! Come, Lord Jesus!
Your grace be with us all! (1 Cor 16:23-24).

~

Blessed be the God and Father
of our Lord Jesus Christ,
a gentle Father and the God of all consolation
who comforts us in all our sorrows! (2 Cor 1:3-4).
The grace of our Lord Jesus Christ,
the love of God the Father,
and the communion of the Holy Spirit
be with us all! (2 Cor 13:13).

~

The grace and peace of God our Father
and the Lord Jesus Christ!
Christ sacrificed himself for our sins
to rescue us from this present wicked world
in accordance with the will of his Father.
God to Christ be glory forever! (Gal 1:3-5).

~

Blessed be the God and Father
of our Lord Jesus Christ,
who has filled us with blessings in Christ! (Eph 1:3-4).

~

Glory to God our Father,
from generation to generation,
in the church and in Christ Jesus! (Eph 3:21).

~

May God the Father and the Lord Jesus
grant peace, love, and faith to all our brothers and sisters!
May grace be with all who love our Lord Jesus Christ! (Eph 6:23-24).

~

May God our Father,
who has begun an excellent work in us,
see that it is finished
when the Day of Christ Jesus comes!
To God be glory forever! (Phil 1:6).

~

May the peace of God that is beyond all understanding
guard our hearts and our thoughts in Christ Jesus! (Phil 4:7).
May God our Father fulfill all our needs
with generosity, with magnificence, in Christ Jesus!
To God be glory forever! (Phil 4:19-20).

~

We give you thanks, our Father!
You call us to share the lot of the saints in light! (Col 1:12).

~

~

You rescue us from the power of darkness
and bring us into the kingdom of your beloved Son (Col 1:13).

~

May the peace of God reign in our hearts,
that peace to which we are called together
as parts of one Body.
In all our words and actions
let us give thanks to God our Father,
in the name of the Lord Jesus (Col 3:15-17).

~

May God our Father put our faith into action,
to work for love, to preserve hope,
through our Lord Jesus Christ (1 Thes 1:2).
May the Lord help us to grow and
abound in love for one another.
May the Lord confirm our hearts in holiness without blame
before God our Father,
at the time of Christ's coming with all the saints (1 Thes 3:12-13).

~

Blessed be God our Father,
who gives salvation through our Lord Jesus Christ.
Christ died and rose again for us
so that, awake or asleep,
we might live together with him (1 Thes 5:9-10).

~

May the Lord of peace
give us peace all the time and in every way!
The Lord be with us all! (2 Thes 3:16).
Grace, mercy, and peace from God our Father
and Christ Jesus, our Lord! (1 Tm 1:2).

~

To the eternal King,
the immortal, invisible, and only God,
be honor and glory forever and ever! (1 Tm 1:17).

~

To the blessed and only ruler of all,
to the King of kings and Lord of lords,
who alone is immortal,
who lives in unapproachable light,
whom no one has ever seen or can see,
to God be honor and everlasting power! (1 Tm 6:15-16).

~

Jesus Christ, the same
yesterday, today, and forever.
To him be glory forever! (Heb 13:8).

~

May God be glorified in all things through Jesus Christ!
To God be glory and power, forever and ever! (1 Pt 4:11).

~

May the God of all grace who has called us
to everlasting glory in Christ Jesus,
after brief suffering,
restore us and confirm us.
May Christ strengthen us and make us steadfast.
To our God be power forever and ever! (1 Pt 5:10-11).

~

May grace and peace be given us in abundance
as we come to know God
and Jesus, our Lord!
Glory be to God forever and ever! (2 Pt 12).

~

May we grow in the grace and knowledge
of our Lord and Savior, Jesus Christ!
Glory be to God now and in eternity! (2 Pt 3:1).

~

To him who can keep you from falling
and bring you safely into God's glorious presence,
innocent and happy,
to the only God, our Savior, through Jesus our Lord,
be glory, majesty, authority, and power,
from even before the beginning of time,
through the present,
and for all ages to come (Jude 24-25).

~

Praise, glory, and wisdom,
thanksgiving, honor, power, and strength,
to our God forever and ever! (Rv 7:12).

~

Amen! Come, Lord Jesus!
May your grace be with us all! (Rv 22:21).

~

NOTES

1. St. John Chrysostom, eighth century.

2. *Gelasian Sacramentary*, eighth century.

3. *The Lucernary*, Apostolic Tradition of Hippolytus, third century.

4. *Kiddush*, Jewish Sabbath blessing.

5. Old Russian Prayer, *Family Festivals*, Resource Publications.

6. Jewish *Tephillah*.

7. St. Francis of Assisi, translated by Benen Fahy, O.F.M., in *Writings of St. Francis of Assisi*, Franciscan Herald Press.

8. Jewish night prayer.

9. Jewish night prayer.

10. Based on the prayer from the *Didache*, second century.

11. Adapted, *Sacramentary*, prayer for the preparation of the gifts.

12. Adapted, *Sacramentary*, prayer for the preparation of the gifts.

13. *Book of Common Prayer*, Episcopal Church.

14. *Praise Him!*, Ave Maria Press, p. 119.

15. *Lutheran Book of Worship*.

16. *Lutheran Book of Worship*.

17. Adapted, *Roman Ritual, Vol. III, The Blessings*, copyright © 1946, Bruce Publishing Co.

18. Adapted, *Roman Ritual, Vol. III, The Blessings*, copyright © 1946, Bruce Publishing Co.

19. *Lutheran Book of Worship*.

20. *Sacramentary*, Christmas Mass at Dawn.

21. *Sacramentary*, Common of Pastors.

22. From *Liturgy 70*, Christmas 1977, with adaptations and additions.

23. Adapted from *Prayers for the Domestic Church*, copyright © 1979 by Rev. Edward M. Hays, Forest of Peace Books, Easton KS 66020.

24. From *Liturgy 70*, Christmas 1977, with adaptations and additions.

25. Adapted from *Prayers for the Domestic Church*, copyright © 1979 by Rev. Edward M. Hays, Forest of Peace Books, Easton KS 66020.

26. *Sacramentary*, Feast of the Holy Family.

27. *Book of Occasional Services*, Episcopal Church.

28. *Lutheran Book of Worship*.

29. Adapted from *Prayers for the Domestic Church*, copyright © 1979 by Rev. Edward M. Hays, Forest of Peace Books, Easton KS 66020.

30. From Office of Liturgy, Diocese of Columbus copyright © 1981. All rights reserved.

31. Adapted from a service written by James E. Wilbur, Paluch Pub. Co., Chicago.

32. *Book of Family Prayer*, Huck, Seabury Press.

33. *Sacramentary*, Solemn Blessing, Passion Sunday.

34. From *The Week with Christ*, William G. Storey, copyright © 1978 Ave Maria Press, Notre Dame, IN.

35. *Sacramentary*, Easter Vigil.

36. *Sacramentary*, Ascension.

37. *Sacramentary*, Pentecost, Vigil Mass.

38. *Sacramentary*, Masses and Prayers for Various Needs and Occasions, For the Blessing of Man's Labor.

39. Adapted, *Lutheran Book of Worship*.

40. *Sacramentary*, All Saints.

41. Adapted, *Rite of Baptism for Children*.

42. *Book of Common Prayer*, Episcopal Church.

43. *Sacramentary*, All Souls.

44. *Book of Common Prayer*, Episcopal Church.

45. *Book of Occasional Services*, Episcopal Church.

46. Adapted, *Book of Occasional Services*, Episcopal Church.

47. *Book of Occasional Services*, Episcopal Church.

48. Worship Resources, Inc., 3015 Zuni Street, Denver, CO 80211.

49. *Book of Occasional Services*, Episcopal Church.

50. *Book of Occasional Services*, Episcopal Church.

51. Adapted, *Book of Occasional Services*, Episcopal Church.

52. *Book of Occasional Services*, Episcopal Church.

53. *Book of Occasional Services*, Episcopal Church.

54. Worship Resources, Inc., 3015 Zuni Street, Denver, CO 80211.

55. Worship Resources, Inc., 3015 Zuni Street, Denver, CO 80211.

56. *Book of Occasional Services*, Episcopal Church.

57. *Book of Occasional Services*, Episcopal Church.

58. *Book of Occasional Services*, Episcopal Church.

59. *Book of Occasional Services*, Episcopal Church.

60. *Book of Common Prayer*, Episcopal Church.

61. Translation, German *Book of Blessings*.

62. *Book of Common Prayer*, Episcopal Church.

63. Adapted, *Rite of Baptism for Children*.

64. Adapted, *Rite of Baptism for Children*.

65. Adapted, Worship Resources, Inc., 3015 Zuni Street, Denver, CO 80211.

66. *Sacramentary*, Anniversary of Marriage.

67. *Book of Common Prayer*, Episcopal Church.

68. *Home Celebrations*, Lawrence Moser, SJ, Paulist Press, 1970.

69. Adapted from text by the Liturgical Commission, Diocese of Lansing.

70. Paraphrase of scripture are based on *Come, Lord Jesus: Biblical Prayers with Psalms and Scripture Readings* by Lucien Deiss, C.S.Sp., World Library Publications, Chicago, 1981, pp. 298-302.